CMU contessions

PERSONALIZE THIS
The role of personalization in the customer lifecycle

&

DISRUPT THAT
Why all marketers need to think like startups do.

Daniel Glickman, CMO

CONTENTS

PERSONALIZE THIS

DISRUPT THAT

CMO confessions

BOOK 1

PERSONALIZE THIS

The role of personalization in the
customer lifecycle

Warning: This Book Has Not Been Personalized

A good book offers a hook; a good business book offers a promise. In the past, all we marketers delivered were hooks and promises. Here's the main thing I've got for you today though, as a CMO in 2016: Questions.

Everywhere I go, I keep running into other CMOs and even CEOs who, like me, are struggling to understand the value of personalization in the customer lifecycle. How can brands benefit from personalization? How do we gain more value and better loyalty? Where do we even begin in our shift toward deeper and more authentic personalization? How can we garner better evangelism from our customers via personalization? Will artificial intelligence take over and render us all worthless?

Okay, the final question is facetious, but the point is—life in the 21st century marketing trenches moves at a futuristic pace. One of the reasons I wrote this book so short is that I know how precious time is. And one of the reasons I'm not promising ninety-nine solutions to your ninety-nine marketing problems is that those lists are easy enough to find online–and I believe you first have to pose questions that are relevant to your company, budget, company culture, and product or service, before any so-called expert wisdom matters.

Questions lead to possibilities. Questions force you to think things through, work sh*t out, and build systems and processes accordingly. Questions allow too, for "failure," even though I'm not a big believer in the existence of failure–certainly not if we are learning and growing in new directions from our mistakes.

In my circle of marketing peers, I'm known for making CMO Confessions. Mostly, I'll admit, I don't have all the answers. And I don't want them. If I thought I knew exactly what customers wanted from brands and when and how they wanted it, I would stop trying to figure humans out–and where's the fun in that?

I work for a successful start up that works with larger, more sophisticated and better funded companies and brands, meaning, I constantly walk that tightrope between seeing how it all is being done by those with deep pockets, and trying to get it all done on a regular budget. I love my job, but I confess–I feel envious. Life isn't fair–we should all be able to plug into the Internet of Things and the mesh and run full-piston algorithms on our data with the talent resources to translate it all into superior customer journeys. We should all be Amazons, but really, the world can't contain one more Amazon–so we run our marketing teams across the tightrope with us.

We disrupt—we walk a thin line and put everyone on edge because we want to do things differently; we take in the broad view—look at that sea of customers and potential customers out there; we put one focused foot in front of the other—marketing entails well-thought out steps; and we remain agile—conditions up here in marketing land change frequently, we test the winds lest we fall out of the game.

I don't have all the answers, but I do have insight and questions that I'd like to share with you in the time it takes to board a train in NYC and arrive in Boston.

Chapter One

Personalization: Relationships Matter

Why do you stick with a friend through thick and thin? In part, because you know each other's bullsh*t and to start new friendships from scratch takes a heap of effort and energy.

Once you begin to know and accept someone–basically, to develop a relationship with them–you become invested, and once you become invested, you make a commitment. Ultimately, it is hard for most of us to back out of something we have put our time, money, word, and possibly heart into.

As marketers, we should keep this in mind: As long as we aim to build and maintain legitimate mutually beneficial and satisfying relationships with our customers, it is most likely that only an egregious error on our part will cause anyone to walk away–to reject us, to smear our good name across social media.

Segmentation, Automation, Personification, and Personalization: Moving Beyond "Dear John" Messaging

In marketing, we basically have run from segmentation and automation, to personification to personalization. In a nutshell, each of these methods allows us to communicate more accurately with our audience, but some methods allow us to be more precise and authentic than ever before. Some allow us, if we "listen" well, to respond to our customers with real-time, context-driven, relationship-building messages.

In segmentation, we create audiences/ segments/ slices/ groups (or whatever you call a portion of your list), and use marketing automation to send out different communications to each group. Today, most serious marketing departments already segment their audiences, but believe it or not, I still come across major brands that don't. I'm not sure what the reasoning in these cases could be, but I do understand that segmentation comes with its challenges.

The main challenge in segmentation is dealing with the "spaghetti" of business logic (or automation rules). For example, at a basic level, the system revolves around something that looks like this:.

> If {user} is (account="premium") and (last login date > 14 days ago) then send {email_id=5555555} else...

Spaghetti logic results in poor communication delivery. By the time you have all that logic built up, you have no idea who receives what email, and when. In fact, some segments could receive six emails per day, and you would be none the wiser. You'd perhaps see people unsubscribing, but wouldn't be quite sure why.

Given the power and user-friendly capabilities of today's data collection technologies, we all have the power to know the who, what, when, where, and why of the majority of marketing decisions we make. Why then, would anyone not take advantage?

Personification attempts to solve the problems segmentation cannot; it is a methodology, not a technology. Applying personification, marketers describe the typical persona types (there are usually four to six), and then build their business logic around them. Personification helps sort out the spaghetti, but does nothing more.

Personalization is a quantum leap forward: It allows businesses to relate to each customer as a segment of one member. Naturally, this results in infinite segments, rendering it impossible to manually write business logic for each individual customer. To achieve a segment of one, you must set the business logic off to the side and automate the automation.

Some believe they are engaging their customers in personalization merely by "adding personal attributes to a communication. They think, for example: that when a customer opens an email and reads: Dear {customer name}, that customer will be impressed—"This company, this brand, really knows me."

Ten years ago, maybe some segments got all starry-eyed over such "personalized" emails; today, "Dear John" emails have become ubiquitous, and most people know it.

Personalization takes modern consumer savvy to heart by building a profile for each and every audience member and customizing every communication, experience, and data presentation to their needs. Personalization reaches far beyond addressing a person by name, or even beyond allowing a client to login to his or her account; personalization revolves around a customer-centric marketing approach.

Getting Personal

Just a few years ago, we began to aim for what we now term personalization, but we really didn't know much about our audience because doing so was still too expensive and unwieldy. Today though, thanks to new technology and advancements in data sciences, not only can we identify segments, but we can also collect real-time behavioral data at deeper and ongoing levels.

Over time, we can build an actual psychological profile of our customers, and then tailor and aim our communications and offers more specifically.

Is our customer a shopper at one of our new locations and/or our fan? Do they tend to shop seasonally, during sales, or piece-by-piece? Do we send them this newsletter, or that one–and on what day or days of the week?

Personalization allows us to get this close to our customers; it allows us to take those first steps toward building a relationship, and then to learn more at each and every touchpoint. Personalization allows for the nurturing of intimacy. And we know that once we humans begin to bond, it becomes harder and harder to walk away.

So, if marketers recognize the power of building customer experiences that foster a deepening win-win commitment over time, why are we still just talking the talk and not quite giving the people what they want? We think it is our job to make consumers anxious–

to leave them always wanting more because they are not quite good enough or cool enough or smart enough, right? The marketer dangles the carrot; the marketer makes believe there is happiness just around the next bend. But let me confess what makes marketers anxious: Forrester Research reports.

Forrester Research revealed that most marketers believe they're doing a better job at personalization than they are. Of the marketers they surveyed in one recent study, two-thirds rated their personalization tactics as "very good" or "excellent." Sounds impressive, right? But of the consumers Forrester surveyed for this same study, only 31% agreed with those high ratings.

This sad statistic supports what I see out in the field on a regular basis: Many marketers say and believe they are personalizing the customer experience, but many are still managing their business, somehow, via segmentation and basic automation. They are sending the same emails out to their top-notch preferred customers as they are to their mediocre ones; or, they are sending too many emails out, or their emails are not reaching customers in real-time and in relevant situations.

True personalization aims to create a unique experience for each and every customer. Savvy customers know true personalization now when they see it. A simple automated "Hello, Daniel" email is no longer enough. Even at their best, segmentation, automation, and personification forget that there is a real person behind each customer.

Personalization asks: What is Daniel's story? It moves beyond merely selling stuff to understanding the way people think about and use your product, service, or brand, while simultaneously molding the way people think about and use your product, service, or brand.

Is the Daniel now calling our customer service line a CMO, or is he a sixty-five year old school teacher just trying to print something on his printer? If he is the latter and we attempt to upsell him, we waste everyone's time. We have lost sight of the whole picture, and I guarantee our lack of clarity will register on the sixty-five year old Daniel's radar.

Getting personal does not mean that you never segment or personify again—we generally don't want to throw the babies out with the bath water. Personification, for example, is widely used in customer experience design, and is a solid system for extracting data about millions of users via a practice we call segment discovery. The point is: There is no excuse for stopping short of doing what is possible now in terms of harnessing data in the name of forging better customer experiences and win-win relationships.

Segments and Rules and Automation, Oh My!

But of course, today I see lots of this blind faith going around: "We're personalizing, see… look at all our data!"

Gathering all the data in the world will do your marketing team no good if nobody knows how to pull it all together, analyze it, and translate it back to the marketing department and entire company—in a relevant and comprehensible way. You cannot simply view your personas via separate silos, i.e. you can't have your customer data split between your CRM, email sendoff system, social media management platform, and/or the fifteen hundred other tools you use. Nor can you simply dump all your data into one data warehouse and declare: "Here's the whole picture."

You must work at making your data relevant dynamically, over time, and in real time. You must deploy what David Edelman refers to as "war-room like scrum teams." You must compile your data, pore over it, merge it, filter it via a system you have pre-built for each product or service you want to make people fall in love with, and then revise, revisit, and re-imagine–constantly.

Still in love with marketing?

Marketing is a long-term relationship that requires marketers not just to translate what we harness via data, and then write up great content and throw it against the wall to see what sticks, it is about understanding context. Where are our consumers now, what are they doing, what device and channel are they engaging with us on, and what do they want now?

A New Business Imperative

Customers want to engage with companies they sense know them. This doesn't happen, of course, overnight–even if a customer fills out one form today in order to take advantage of your free eBook, you've still only got the basics. But the point is, the longer you can keep your customers interested and engaged, the more they will share with you, and the better the value you will be able to provide– and so the cycle will go, turning in on itself in tighter and tighter circles that will allow both you and your customers to squeeze out even more value.

Look at how Barnes and Noble has struggled and lost, not only because Amazon has crushed them online, but because they continued for too long to rely on segmentation. They tried to sell the so-called "Number One" books, by placing them all on one large table in front of the store, in piles constructed along rough segment lines (YA fan, romance fan, vampire fan, outdoor adventure fan). They labeled these books Top Sellers, but these were picks that did not–that could not–take into account the type of high resolution that personalization delivers.

Your small local bookstore clerk could do better than the staff at Barnes and Noble, because over time, they could see what books you chose and could chat with you. They were invested in you in ways Barnes and Noble staff was not. Mom and Pop could make recommendations. Amazon does the same. Barnes and Noble took on Mom and Pop bookstores because they had the power of scale, but when Amazon offered all that plus the personal approach they crushed Barnes and Noble.

Barnes and Noble style segmentation said, "Let's try to push a book at a person that fits this general persona."

Personalization says, "Let's try to help this person find the books they love."

Personalization can be–and is–just as fundamental and deep online as it was in that old tiny bookstore you have so much nostalgia for. One reason we keep running back to Amazon is because Amazon does know us just like Mom and Pop did, and it continues to know us better.

One-click shopping and tailor-made suggestions based on what we've already purchased, viewed, favorited, or saved for later, saves us time and effort. Yes, I should go into town and check out other places this week, but my Amazon page is bookmarked and organized, and besides, I don't want to have to drive and park, or sign up elsewhere. The time it takes for another vendor to get to know me and my preferences, and for me to get to know and relate to them? I don't have it!

It sounds ludicrous, but we do find comfort in familiarity and we can get emotionally attached to a brand. In today's first-world experience economy, people will pay for comfort, convenience, and emotional feel-good.

Would you love to switch cable or phone companies? Sure, but what a pain in the neck. You are committed (literally). If you are like most people, you are not actually loyal to your cellular or cable provider, you just know their bullsh*t. If it were easy (and cheap), you would switch to any competitor who offered you even a slightly better deal. Cable and phone companies know this, and so they keep coming up with more and more tricks to force you to say with them.

When done right, a personal approach would look exactly the opposite of these wicked models! The old push marketing approach is all about luring the customer into a deal, personalization allows you to become alluring.

Zooming In for the Long Haul

Personalization works on basic human psychological principles– once your customers are "in," you have to really screw up to make them stray.

Personalization engages customers by providing:

- A deep relationship that goes far beyond persona: i.e. beyond Hank is a married white male who lives in the 90210 zip code with his wife and three children. This relationship makes customers feel like you truly "get them," and in fact, for the most part, you do!

- Real time and dollar savings, such as points earned, 5% back, free shipping, and one-click checkout.

- Added value through data shared, that is, customers are willing to divulge more and more personal information with you over time, as long as that sharing adds up to the benefit of you delivering goods and services to them the way Mom and Pop would have.

We could also say that personalization is about these three things:

- **Relevancy** - Always (and only) providing the most relevant services, content, options, and support.

- **Intimacy** - Knowing (and having the permission to know) things that are very personal such as location, habits, preferences, and interests in order to be more relevant.

- **Dialogue** - Intimacy isn't fostered by passively collecting information. Cultivate a dynamic "above the board" relationship where you and your customer happily exchange information for relevancy and service.

The fact is, even younger generation consumers who have never set foot in a Mom and Pop store of any kind, crave the feeling those experiences brought those of us above a certain age. Age has nothing to do with the human urge to feel known, to belong, and to be valued.

So if you continue to look at personalization simply as a very high-resolution segmentation methodology, you will be missing out. True personalization is a manifestation of a customer-centric marketing approach, and putting the customer in the center can lead to major improvements in business KPIs, by bringing about the following:

- An increase in customer lifetime value (cLTV).
- An emotionally captive audience that is less likely to churn.
- An increase in fanfare and word-of mouth marketing (Viral Factor).
- A decrease in customer support calls and increase in NPS.

So, how do you figure out a strategy that will lead to stronger personalization? How will you break through the worrisome Forrester Research statistics to deliver consumers what they are asking for?

Begin by asking yourself the following questions:

1. How will your customers benefit from a personalized service?
2. How will they perceive their relationship with you to be more personal?
3. How will the data and the customized service you are

providing keep them dedicated to you? Or, how will you keep them from making the effort they never want to have to make to ditch you for somebody else?

Once you get good at the personalization game, then what? How do you gain the competitive advantage? Eventually, Netflix is going to hit the glass ceiling—they will know all they need to know about your taste in TV shows and movies. When a competitor finds a way to collect all the data Netflix has, and can make the time, effort, and dollar cost to switch services zero, they will score. But how could they do that?

The knowledge you have about your customers can be your best defense against the competition, but only if you use it to create a relationship with your customers—a relationship that the younger, sexier, newer model will have a hard time competing with.

Still in love with marketing?

WAYZ is. WAYZ already knows how to push the personalization envelope in the traffic app game: the more details I give up, the more on it they are for me. They know where I work Monday through Friday from 8:00 a.m. to 6:00 p.m., and they'll send me a message: Leave ten minutes earlier than usual today, there's been an accident at Mass Ave. I might eventually tell WAYZ where I lift weights, where my kids go to school, and what my family's favorite weekend public spaces to visit are, because we will reap the benefits— we'll get to where we need or want to be on time and will be more productive, successful, and relaxed!

Whatever product, service, or brand you are marketing—you have a chance to build an even stronger relationship to your market. Take just ten minutes to reflect on your various experiences as a customer and flip all of that onto your own plate: How will you steer that first "meeting" toward a courtship that is mutually fun, exciting, and rewarding–toward a personalized bond that is continually expanding and solidifying at the same time? How will you show your customers that you are continually making the effort to make their lives better?

Chapter Two

Data for Personalization: Crunch, Review, and Render Relevant

Personalization relies heavily not just on data, but also on big data, big data crunching, and big automation; it demands a whole new level of automation of actions.

Marketers can no longer rely on "If this, then that" logic.

We are far beyond a mere reworking of the old formula: "The email has already been written, when should I send it?"

Those who embrace customer centric marketing understand the value of taking a quick pause (in tech time–not even a millisecond) to "look at" the person we're about to shoot an email to, which then triggers the software to review that person's profile and not only figure out when to send that email, but what specific pieces of content should fill which specific sections of that email.

Voila!

Of course, it isn't always simple. Sometimes you know next to nothing about a person, and sometimes you have some basic segmentation-level information on them. Other times, you are dealing with a loyal lifelong customer. No matter the case, it's not the personalization in itself that is new; it's the data. We have access to more relevant and timely data, we have the technology to process that data, and the technology is becoming more tailored and affordable to businesses of all types and sizes.

The challenge in gaining the competitive advantage via your data lies in understanding how to:

- Classify and collect it.
- Structure it.
- Use it to predict (to fill in the gaps).

Classify: Raw Versus Processed Data

There are two different levels of information in systems analysis: One is just raw data–time of day, number of followers, what brand did they purchase, when was the last time they called in, when is their subscription due? This data is a number of some sort, or text. On its own, it means very little.

The other type of data is data that we have to figure out, or process. Is this woman a businessperson, and if so, is she an influencer in her industry? This "beyond data" data is insight, and that insight becomes its own piece of data.

But always, the first step is to collect the data.

Data is scattered throughout the business. Typically, once a prospect is "handed over" from one company silo to another, a lot of data is lost: consider all the data the marketing department collected about the lead before they purchased. 9 times of 10, the vast majority of that data is lost because the individual person is now stored in a different database.

There is also a problem when a company collects a heck of a lot of data, but that data isn't accessible to the personalization expert—or when it is too dispersed across the organization. Here's just a short list of types of data that can slip through the cracks:

- What URLs did the contact visit recently? (i.e. Did they try to fill out that upgrade form only to abandon it?)
- Customer support tickets
- Email behavior
- Social activity
- Articles read
- CRM data
- MAP data
- Call center data
- Third party data
- Customer input into interactive content
- Survey results

And what kind of "insight" data can go unmined, if the right people–these days, that means everyone in the company–don't see it? If you don't put the pieces together quickly and coherently, you risk losing data that can be inferred from behavior:

- Interest: The more a user engages with content of a certain topic, the more interest they express in it.

- Intent: Certain types of content and digital properties may indicate intent. These include: forms, contact us, request info pages, find a location, manuals, etc. (Think about your equivalent to the "Add to cart" button on an e-commerce site.)

- Adoption rate: How quickly has this customer reacted to calls to action in the past.

- Personal data: Create interactive content that is designed to learn more about the person, for example: reviews, ratings, quizzes and so on. Get   them to add this data to their profile, or do it for them.

- Financial ability: Have they purchased luxury items in the past? Do they   have a credit card on file? Have they been clipping your coupons?

- Buyer type: Impulse buyer, or careful comparer?

The RFM model is probably still one of the best models out there to determine the customer's potential value: Recency, Frequency, and Monetization. The higher the customer scores on each of these variables, the more potential they have to provide you with more value. Do not miss out on this data. If one of your customers scores high on RFM, what could you do to upsell/cross sell them? If they score low, what could you do to re-engage them?

Clearly, we can go pretty far with data, and we can also go crazy! But generally, now, raw data is not what interests marketers. Now, I'd go so far to say, for most types of business, using raw data alone brings lackluster results.

Most marketers understand that powerful analytics is crucial to getting and staying above the fray. Some level of intelligence must take our data and crunch it into something we can base our decisions on. When we have a whole lot of data, we need a whole lot of dynamic, fast-processing intelligence. Automation comes into play here, but it isn't where the buck stops.

The buck still stops with humans. We try our best to structure our automation in ways that align with our goals, the automation spits out data that matters most, we connect the data dots and act on them, and then we start to see progress in the form of making inroads with customers that is based on actual insight—not just on segments, numbers, or if/thens.

Think about what data you have to collect. If you have way too much, weed it out by imagining that you could know anything you ever wanted to know about your customer or prospect. How would you influence their behavior? That is: How would you personalize the experience to get them to buy better, or to re-engage with you, or to purchase something new? Answer these questions, and then reverse engineer the system.

Here's a quick template for a worksheet:

Data	Purpose	Method of collection	Possible values
Gender	Include / exclude feminine products	Signup form	Male Female
Social influence score	To suggest social sharing	3d party API	1-100
Current plan	To determine best upsell possibilities	CRM	"Sports", "Sports Plus", Etc.
Is a coupon seeker	Offer coupons prior to renewal date	Visits to discount related pages, Affiliates, CRM (has coupon been applied), Call center logs	True/False

Structure

The biggest sources of data that are not used properly are the ones where the prospect tells you something about themselves–they provide signals and opportunities that you don't act properly (or fast enough) on.

In order to determine how interested somebody is in a certain topic, we might ask them to fill out our sleek online form, but many times, we present them with nothing more than the following: "Welcome back! Download our amazing e-book for free, and in exchange we'll ask you just a few (of the same) questions (we asked last time)."

There isn't just one research team reporting on how we marketers are fooling ourselves, and not fooling our customers. A multitude of studies show that while we believe we are impressing and wooing the masses, in reality, customers find our efforts "old-fashioned," not creative or compelling enough, and unrelated to their interests and preferences. That is, despite all of our access to all of their data, we are still not nailing what matters most to our customers.

The human dimension comes first—the story, the journey—whatever you want to call it—but these days, it cannot come without fully integrating and translating the data.

How many signals—in the form of data—are you receiving today that are being picked up by your marketing automation or personalization systems, but that are not being tied to other notes, and acted upon? Tying it all together is the challenge and one of the main ways to gain the competitive edge: Data that is fragmented or not in the right place at the right time, is not actionable.

When I'm asked what data is used for personalization, I answer: "All of it, and not that much of it. It depends what stage of the customer lifecycle you're at."

You get their address, their income to debt ratio, and other pieces of information that are available in public records. We can also look things up via LinkedIn, Klout, and Facebook. We can, of course, buy data. Sometimes you have a few behavioral pieces of data, like a person's browsing history. Did they visit your site before, or this page of your site before?

Always, you are relying on different data from different sources and parts of the lifecycle, and using it to inform strategy; but again, during any stage of the customer lifecycle, different data is relevant. What data am I going to use and when is it most relevant?

Below is a cheat-sheet for determining what data to collect at what stage, and how. To put a proper personalization plan into motion, you will need to break this table down into great detail and share it between all departments. That is, your content marketer needs to know to create an interactive calculator that captures certain data, while your email marketer needs to know to direct traffic there at the proper stage.

Customer lifecycle stage	Behavioral	Forms	Interactive	3d Party
Visitor	Page visits	-	-	Basic HTTP data
Prospect	Product interest	Simple Signup forms	-	Social login data
Buyer	interest level	Lead-gen forms	ROI calculators, product selection guides	Influencer score.
Customer - early stages	Product engagement, Technical documentation usage	setup wizards	-	-
Customer - well known	NPS, frequency of usage. behavioral change, support contacts	surveys	best practices guide	-

Databases and systems must talk to each other. We need to structure and format our data to make it useful. A link click is just a link click, but if we know the link's significance, we can parse and reformat the data and store it in the customer profile. Markup languages such as AMPL provide a nice starting point to understand the logic behind such a system.

Here's what this would look like in action:

Data in the data warehouse:

GID=1234556, url, "http://www.mysite.com/randompage", date, 1/12/2016, time, 03:43, duration, 1.45.

Data after parsing and reformatting in the personal profile:
Days since last visit: 2.

Personal profile data should always be actionable data, and it should always be up-to-date.

But even data that is properly formatted (like the example above) hides locked within it even more actionable data. This kind of data has to do with patterns you find inside the warehouse. For-example: Is this person more likely than average to take advantage of offers? Do they love to read books, or articles? Are they a happy and loyal customer? Or, are they nearing a purchase decision? To unlock this data we need to be able to predict.

Predict

How do we use the data to figure out what to do next? This is where Big Data comes into play.

The term Big Data is somewhat ambiguous, but it usually refers to the ability to store, crunch, and analyze massive amounts of data collected from large populations.

How do you gain personal insights from a massive database? Generally, there are three different types of analyses that personalization experts in a business can run:

1. Statistical clusters in the matrix.
   What does this user have in common with other users that may have the same (or similar) characteristics? This could be a good way to complete information when a user's profile is incomplete. Of course, you will want to constantly improve your data and verify any assumptions you have with your users. Smart personalization means that you routinely look for such signals using questioners, heart buttons, and engagement metrics. For example: The system may notice that a customer has a lot in common with single moms. A question might come up in a survey to confirm this assumption: "Help us improve our service. Would you be interested in…?"

2. Contextual categorization.
   URLs and serial numbers are just those, but if we provide context to these elements by using our CMS, GTM, or hard code, we can discover patterns and correlations, and can learn more about what items are consumed by whom. We can then take action, and suggest more of the same. Keep in mind though, your CMS, GTM, and hard code must be thoroughly thought through first: You can't successfully count on offering more 70s girl band rock hits if your content was not tagged as such in the first place.

3. Context of the user's activity and content consumed.
A long-term customer may have recently visited your pricing page and contact page, and then she viewed some technical documentation. The first two visits might signal intent, while the third signals interest. Proper analysis of the data should flag this customer as one who is thinking of upgrading. They are moving into the next step of the customer lifecycle in plain view—can we see them?

We will probably always run A/B tests and big data will probably always get bigger. Our tech will crunch more data and will draw more statistical correlations. Now, with e-commerce for instance, we're tapped into a logic that works (for Amazon, anyway), that is: There is a high correlation between people who like one thing and people who like another.

But there will also always be non-correlative outliers—the hard-to-pin-down. Music is an exception. It's highly personal and nuanced. The fact that I, Daniel, like a specific 80s song doesn't necessarily mean that I'm an 80s person. Using the "People who like this will also like that" does not always work here. There is no logic that always works.

How do we gain insight that will lead us toward personalization anyway?

All we might know about this customer, Daniel (who loves the 80s love song from the movie Ghost), is where he is from and maybe a couple of pages he has visited. If he's a fairly regular customer, we've had the opportunity to ask him a hundred questions and to look at what he's purchased. We know quite a bit. We know that

Daniel has $3.2 million in mortgage debt and owns five antique cars. He subscribes to Private Island Online.

The mom and pop at the mom-and-pop store, who knew Daniel, would start building a psychological profile of him. The more interactions and conversations they had with him, the more they'd get to know him–that is, they would understand more than "just Daniel's behavior." They would know that he liked that song from Ghost because his cousin wrote the lyrics. In general though, mom and pop know Daniel's a blues and country rock guy, because he has talked to them about it.

We are now entering an era where your personalization system can do what mom and pop did: You can use your data to build an actual psychological profile of your customer. It's typically done at the very low end of the funnel or with existing consumers, and dwelling here can bring you benefits, but also trouble, such as when a company put its data together and concluded: "This girl is pregnant. Let's send her coupons for formula and diapers, via snail mail." Then, the parents she still lived with opened the mailbox and... Uh oh! The pregnancy had not been planned.

Here is how data used to work

1. Customer buys more skin care products than usual (specifically, more stretch mark cream)

2. System sends this person more coupons of products that are statistically related

Now we are a bit more sophisticated:

1. *Customer buys more skin care products (stretch mark cream) than normal*

2. *System deducts that the person is pregnant*

3. *System looks up purchases and needs of other pregnant women and sends these coupons or products*

Our level of sophistication improves every day, and ultimately, Artificial Intelligence (AI) might take over the bulk of the process. But no matter what, your system needs to be more discrete when the pregnant woman is very young, as privacy issues play a bigger role. As of now, no AI system will know this by itself, so it's always good to seek customer input for predictive profiling.

Predictive profiling can be done by asking a direct question, or by making gradual changes in terms of offers and content delivered, while measuring the engagement level changes that result. For example:

Customer buys more skin care products (stretch mark cream) than normal, so:

1. *System deduces that the person is pregnant.*

2. *System looks up purchases and needs of other pregnant woman.*

3. *System shows more pregnancy-related content to the woman.*

4. *System gauges engagement level with the new content and increases offers accordingly.*

In other words: Just because someone watched a football game, you can't assume that they just became a sports fan. But being able to label someone as pregnant or sports fan has obvious benefits, and your marketing team should be all over how to extract more value from these types of customers.

Clearly, CMOs have the tools and access to insight now to move their teams past, "Oh, this happened, so let's do that."

Between descriptive systems and top-end proactive systems, we can work all other levels: We can mix-and-match and merge descriptive, diagnostic, analytical, predictive, and proactive elements of our systems in order to create meaningful customer experiences.

We can structure our data and our data systems for maximum agility, so that we do not drop the ball: We can collect, transfer, share, and translate all relevant notes at the right time so we act on the opportunity that the person who visited us in the trade fair booth yesterday gave us. "I've loved your company for ten years," they said.

We don't crush them the next day by sending them a "regular" templated email asking them whether they would like a product demo. (This is such a common mistake, and one that is a big no-no in my book). We may be a real live human, worn out at the end of the day from the trade show, but we get that information node about that particular conversation into whatever database we need to that night—and the customer who has loved us for ten years already, will continue to love us for ten more, because the next day he'll receive an email that says, "Thanks for coming to the booth yesterday and sharing your enthusiasm."

Do we type that line in ourselves? Maybe yes, maybe it's automated. But we win.

Apply: What, Where, and When

We win when we begin to parse what matters most, and when. We know when things must be done manually (maybe we do type a personal email to special clients). We know when things can and must be automated.

We recognize there are certain types of data that are relevant at certain touch points and some that are not. For instance, you can determine very easily what the weather is like at X-person's location right now. You know if it is night or day. But is that relevant data, right now?

Sometimes it is, sometimes it isn't. If one travel company notes the last-minute purchase of an airplane ticket, and this ticket has been purchased because of a death in the family, how might offering up coupons for local Happy Hour hot spots sit with that traveler? Not well, obviously. But if another travel company has collected, somehow, just one more piece of data and either sits back and does nothing at this difficult moment, or offers a discount on some type of self-care service (such as therapy or relaxation massages)–imagine the relationship that might spark.

I worked with one of our own customers–a very big service provider–and we were looking at the data and the different personality types they had to address, trying to figure out how they were going to personalize the customer experience.

A senior marketer asked, "How are we going to find the time to create this many pieces of content for this many people?"

She was looking at sixteen personas with sub-permutations in each, over four different products and twelve different customer touchpoints. That's a lot of permutations.

She was still thinking that she was going to have to do this manually somehow, but I said, "You should expect systems to create X-number of versions of content for each of your sixteen main personas. All you have to do is create some templates, then let the computer do the manual labor."

I helped move this client beyond "segmentation thinking," to the realization that when you have a true personalization system in place, you don't need to create multiple versions of the same rules for different personas: One set of rules can be adapted to infinite segments.

The big question is, once again and ultimately: What data will you need to collect, format, and analyze to setup your rules?

Chapter Three

Why Personalize?

Relate or Perish

When Apple first came out with "always on" Siri or Apple TV, people were a little freaked out: Is that robot going to be listening to me all the time? Does that Apple TV watch me? But over time, people got used to it. They liked the benefits. People love their mobile apps because of all their personalization features. Even BITMOJI allows us to text in "personalized emoji," because emoji is no longer enough.

Personalization is happening, and is developing quite fast. It's already become the new standard. Recently, I got an email from IBM. I was using one of their software programs, and when I was asked to fill out a satisfaction form, I noted that honestly I was not too happy, and then gave some detailed feedback. A week later, I received an email from a product manager. He acknowledged my dissatisfaction then asked for more feedback. I thought: Okay, that's a good personalized email. In the second email he sent a day later, however, he wrote: What product are you using? I'd like to get this to the right person."

That's when I felt stupid, and then mad. I had spent my time doing something for him, assuming we were engaging in a personalized experience. He should have known what product I was using.

This kind of second-rate effort at personalization was completely acceptable just a few years ago. You'd call a 1-800 number and a computerized voice would ask you to enter your account number. It would respond: "Sorry, Daniel, I did not understand. Please enter your account number again." So, you would, and then once you were transferred to a human, he or she would ask you to provide your account number yet again.

There were plenty of technical reasons why first-rate personalization was so difficult to implement just a few years ago, and we were used to it being what it was–sloppy, inefficient, and annoying. That was the reality then; it is not the reality now. We're very used to things being done–and done well–for us. If we aren't entirely used to it quite yet, we at least expect it, because most of us have dealt with at least one company that provides supreme personalized customer service.

The battle to win wishy-washy customers

Interestingly enough, the increase in customer expectation–that we marketers are going to "get them" and treat them special–is happening in parallel with a decrease in brand loyalty. People are not as loyal to brands as they were. Ten years ago, you bought from

Sony and said, "Sony's good. I'm going to keep buying all my electronics products from them." Now, you're going to buy what's cheaper on Amazon. You may not completely trust Brand X, maybe you can't even locate the country that product is made in on a map, but because you trust Amazon–sold! In fact, some of the top selling items on Amazon are made by virtually unknown brands.

Customers expecting more sophisticated personalization efforts, yet being less loyal than ever means two things for marketing departments: First of all, companies are wasting their money, especially if they are sending direct mail that's not personal. Coupons are not personalized and people toss them out immediately. Secondly, with the decrease in brand loyalty, we are playing constant catch up. It's a constant battle to win wishy-washy customers. Even cable and phone companies are experiencing a higher customer turnover than they used to.

Again, Forrester Research shows consumers want and expect more of what we somehow are failing to deliver. Consumers are declaring that they would pay more attention to loyalty programs and loyalty rewards, if companies were offering them greater value. Marketers need to acknowledge that they are working in a new environment, where the old way of building brand loyalty through brand recognition has become way too expensive. Marketers must seek innovative ways to build brand loyalty. In this experience economy we are now a part of, a perception of value is earned, not bought; and loyalty is won by action, not ad spend.

The Collective Mindspace

Nowadays, Google, Siri, the social networks–a lot of search tools–

are influenced by how much the "bigger connective consumer mind" is thinking about you. How much is it talking about you? How many of its neurons are firing around your brand?

If you are not in the collective mindspace, personalization is one of the tools you need to deploy to get there. Engaged customers get those neurons going. Today, you must be visible. If you aren't, you're essentially one of those barber shops that you still sometimes see with the swirly colored pole out front. There are only old men in those shops and old black combs in jars filled with a sickly-colored liquid. You don't want to become one of those old barber shops.

If you don't keep up in the personalization and engagement race, your customers will quickly get the feeling your company or your brand is old, or perhaps worse, that you don't care that you're old, or you don't care enough about them to make an effort. Either way, you become unattractive.

There's no excuse for this type of unattractiveness! We've got tech and AI on our side. We have to think of our company, our service, our brand, and our relationships with our audiences as a question of "Am I attractive?"

Ask yourself right now, just like you would before going on a first date with a potential perfect match, "Am I attractive?" and remember that the marketer's holy grail is emotional engagement, but you may have to ensure that you are physically attractive before you can get there.

NIKE is one of the best examples of taking personalization and emotion to the maximum mindspace level. NIKE invented running. They created this whole concept and movement around "I run."

Their shoes fuel the emotional concept: "I am fast. I am a runner. I'm attractive and strong and good looking." Even if you're jogging just as slow as you've always jogged, no—with NIKE you are a runner! You don't even have to wear NIKE shoes or be a runner, the name and the logo take up that mindspace. It has for decades now. You see the swoosh on the undershirt collar of an MLB player, and you are subconsciously part of NIKE and athletics and all the healthy things associated with that ecosystem. You are fast!

And of course, NIKE doesn't stop there. Running apps may be a dime a dozen now, but NIKE was one of the first companies to push the envelope in this domain. Their running app, for some, is less about the running, and more about feeling good in the running shoes and about being part of the running or sports community. Their app lets you check the local weather so you can plan the best time and route to jog—I mean, to run! Then, of course, it helps you share your workout with your friends and the entire world. You get invited to competitions.

NIKE really kicked ass with personalization. Adidas, on the other hand, went for the old style marketing. Adidas makes good shoes, but if you want to be a runner, which brand is more emotionally engaging? There's no question about it: NIKE rules the collective mindspace.

It all comes down to the notion of getting people to want to buy your product. The goal is to get people to want to wear your logo and to be proud of being part of your community or of being a customer; it's not just to push sales to them. Happy customers ultimately bring you more value.

From providing value to being a valuable partner

The value you can offer your customers will come in different forms. There's the simplest form of value: Amazon, for instance, has the deal of the day, which customers expect to be personally tailored. Amazon knows I'm looking for patio furniture, so they set out some deals: Hello Daniel, go for it. This is a win-win deal, but it isn't necessarily the best win-win deal for either side, because it means the brand is selling cheaper stuff instead of upselling me. I become "the bargain hunter" now, when in reality, both of us would rather have a relationship where I'm a premium payer-upper.

Apple, of course, plays the premium angle. Buying Apple makes you part of the cool club. You pay more to be part of their ecosystem. You're fine with the fact that Apple rarely offers deals and this keeps "bargain hunters" out.

Nordstrom is upselling too. They always have, but with the acquisition of Trunk Club, they're taking the idea of the personal shopper/concierge to the max. You pick a few fashion items you like, Nordstrom creates your style, and every month you get a trunk of goodies that you are "inclined" to like. Whatever you don't like, you send back with the trunk and the algorithms refine and predict from there. Talk about personalization and building loyalty: After a few trunk exchanges, how could any customer go through a similar process of photo-sorting, form-filling, ordering, trying on, returning, and customizing to that level—with any other similar service?

Hilton works personalization in an interesting way: If you are booking a room through their app, you can choose a specific room from a map—the way you purchase theater or concert tickets. It may not seem like a big deal, but how nice it is to snag that corner room, or the one furthest from the elevator. In some hotels, you can choose the firmness of your mattress beforehand. How do they do that—do they have a storage room full of mattresses and two employees who are dedicated solely to moving them around? I don't know and I don't care, these hotels just do it and I never have to sleep in a bed that feels like a marshmallow or a table in a morgue. While traveling all day, this "future" personalized ease and comfort rests at the back of my mind.

Earning prime real estate in this consumer mindscape is all about solving customer problems. If you are able to fit your product in and around the customer's need, you build personalization systems that function in real time—or via what is sometimes called just-in-time marketing.

Understand the context of what it is this customer wants right now, and what their intent is, and you can engage and relate.

You don't have to be as big as NIKE and Apple. Your systems don't have to be as complex. But you do have to take the customer lifecycle into account and push beyond simply pushing for the sale. At the end of the day, it's about people and relationships. You have to plan what you're doing. If you want to attract the bargain shoppers, go for it. If you want to form an exclusive club, be my guest. But one thing I've seen many small businesses and startups fail to understand is this:

In general, the more a customer pays: the happier they are, the more they will talk about you, the more they will be loyal, the more mindspace you'll fill, and the more you will profit.

Robots versus Phonies: Marketing WWIII, The Quest for Even Deeper Personalization

Do we lose anything personal with all this data and technology and soon, with more AI, or can we actually create the same emotion and develop relationships with our customers, using all these tools, the way our old corner diner waitress did with us?

Yes we can: This is the cutting edge of personalization, and I always joke about how navigation systems should have a temperament. Instead of saying, "At the next intersection, turn left. Turn left," they should have attitude. "Daniel, don't forget to turn left. Daniel, you idiot, you just missed your turn!"

They can see me; they know what's going on. I'm distracted and they know I've missed that left turn before. The computer and I joke, we trade a kind of relationship. Of course, nobody knows how to perfect this emotional trade yet with computers, or if they do, it's far too expensive for us common marketers right now. But KFC in China is now staffed by a popular and charming chicken loving robot.

Think about it!

It's got a bit of a personality. It talks. It delights people. We know it's not a human being, but it turns out that people can have a relationship with AI.

Personalization is about emotions and relationships. What we do not want, and what we can now spot from a mile away, is phoniness. Robots cannot be phony–they are artificial. Humans can be phony, and when they are chit chatting with us solely for a tip, our radar screams. When their chit chat takes place in the wrong place or the wrong time, our skin crawls.

When I call customer support at my bank, occasionally I have to wait for a file review. I noticed recently on one call that the person on the other end was chit chatting with me. I wondered: Why am I enjoying this casual conversation? What the heck is going on? Then I realized that they've hit a level of personalization right there, because they never push other services or products, and they never ramble on at the expense of time. If I've put in a request that will take one minute, I'm informed it will take one minute, and in the meantime, we will have this short conversation. I know my bank's marketing team did a lot of work on "finding the appropriate level of chat" because they nailed it. It was a pleasure to talk to the person on the other end of the line. There was nothing off-putting or phony about it.

You can create emotions and seek emotional engagement through light friendly human-to-human conversation, or via a really nice automated but "unique" email. As long as you somehow show that somebody cares, even if it's the computer that cares—you send your customers the message that the brand is putting an effort into not only being attractive, but into them too.

Artificial intelligence is, by definition, a fast learner, and I am a fan of science fiction, but I'm not making this up: If you, as a CMO, are not thinking to some extent about what AI means for your future marketing plan, or how AI could fit into your company at some point, you are way behind. We've seen that when technology kicks in, it moves fast. Not learning what you need to learn today puts your behind in terms of the competitive advantage.

What can AI do for you? Consider the following possibilities:

1. What personalization projects did we shelf because they demanded too much manpower? AI can solve that.

2. What brilliant idea is blooming, but being shot down for seeming simply impossible in terms of time needed for researching each individual customer? AI can do cover this ground.

3. What hidden segments and interesting trends/correlations are we missing out on? AI can discover these.

The fact is, the CMO of 2026 might have a smaller staff than you do–he or she will be armed with one very productive AI.

Attention: Do Not Flood Your Touchpoints

As a marketer, you always want to work on creating more touchpoints. Maybe it's as simple as creating and then promoting your Facebook presence; maybe you need an app.

What you also need is to figure out is how you will maximize every single touchpoint. This does not mean you throw the kitchen sink at your customers at every single touchpoint and see what sticks. Consumers are currently feeling overwhelmed. Your most effective tactic could be spending more time with the customer, or more depth with the customer, whatever works for you–and for them.

Personalization means delivering relevant content at relevant times, so try to build a customer profile, or a preferences profile, and to understand their intent. Ideally, you'll try to figure out their psychology. Maybe this customer is a slow adopter and needs time adopting your product. They don't want to be bothered every three days with, "Hey, start using our product! Have you tried it? Tell us what you think!" They need validation, security, and time. Give them this.

Or, maybe they're excitable. Or motivated by social experiences.

We can figure all this out. We can build our systems almost as a series of "traps," with the main purpose of gaining insight into the client's intent and psychology.

Bill Jones signs up for a cable service, for example. We at the cable company don't know much about Bill at this point, but we do know some. He signed up for the TV+ account, so it seems he's more interested in television than in movies. He's twenty-three and single. This is data we have because we acquired it. It's very basic.

We send Bill an email and build a little experience for him around "typical young guy" shows. If we're smart, we measure how he responds. Then, we go deeper on whatever crumbs we're thrown. We use tags and measure response time and activation time. After the email did he go and check out something we recommended? Did he rate it with two stars or five? Then, beyond email, did Bill hook up the box to the Internet like the instructions said? When should we try to upgrade him?

The question is: How do we create a series of little experiences for customers and track behavior in order to figure out their personality and what stage in the customer lifecycle they are at? It's highly complex, but it's not impossible.

Take Starbucks: How could a coffee shop learn more about their customers in order to become more up-close and personal with them, while ultimately increasing customer value? Before Starbucks came up with their app, this dual goal seemed somewhat unreasonable, but we know now the company is crushing it with same store appearances. The app was designed to make customers' lives easier, for example, by cutting lines and offering discounts. From the marketer's perspective, the app was designed to learn about each individual customer's habits and preferences, and to encourage behaviors that profit Starbucks. That's marketing in the 21st century, and AI will one day do all of this so much better.

In the meantime, we can master this—or, we can at least learn to hold back the floods and engage with our customers on a balanced and deeply personalized level. If we map our touch points out, we can map too, for example, where which customers want more, or want less—we can take action based on "customer maturity." This is what a customer-centric system looks like. It is not a series of fixed touchpoints, it is data that lives and breathes. That's the nuts and bolts of it: You have to have something that manages customer communications in one center spot, based on all incoming signals. You then have to analyze these signals and respond—pronto.

Get With the Personalization Program, Folks!

The vast majority of companies are still working their advanced segmentation methodologies. I've said it before: The problem with advanced segmentation is that it creates so much more labor than is now necessary, and delivers diminishing results.

When the need to truly figure out personalization is brought up, I hear this again and again from marketing departments: But taking it to the next level is highly technical. Our web team is a totally different team from our email team. We don't have analytics, so we have no clue what happens after someone clicks an email. It's wishful thinking to be able to ask different questions each time different people hit our landing page. It's too silo-ed, it's too crazy!

It all sounds cliché and true–and it may be–but so is this: You really have to swap your whole marketing approach on its head. Flip your departments and say, "Fine then! Let's do this backwards. Instead of continuing to do what we're doing and trying to do it better, let's clearly define what we want to do, and then reorganize ourselves to get it done."

It may sound too simple and may not be simple–but what is? Be disruptive, flip yourself. Go backwards. Too many departmental issues or hoops or differences? Why not shut up and say what you want and then keep chiseling away until you've got a way to get there. It's smart and difficult. It's really not vague or cliché after all; it's like come on–no excuses.

*

Back in the 50s, people really cared what their neighbors were doing. If that's true today, we don't like to admit it. We don't like to think of ourselves as fitting in–we're special. We deserve the VIP gold glove treatment. Of course, we're not special and don't deserve a thing. This is not Lake Wobegon, where all the kids are above average, all the men are handsome, and all the women are strong.

But if we look at our customers as something akin to a channel–we can retain them, sell to them again, upsell them, and give them the

VIP sensation. We can get them to evangelize for us. Personalization is a major tool in managing this customer "channel." Manage it accordingly, have the same KPIs and metrics as you do with any other channel, and invest in it appropriately–in some cases, invest in it much more than you do in other channels, because you'll get a lot more out of it. Instill in your teams this line of thinking and you will go far.

Ask yourself: What is our strategy for marketing through our customers? Most of your competitors probably don't have a strategy, so if you have a large number of customers or if your customers are highly influential, such a channel would make one hell of a competitive advantage.

Chapter Four

The Role of Personalization in the Customer Lifecycle

The customer lifecycle approach applies specifically to companies that have–or that want to have–a complex relationship with their customers. It starts with the understanding that the goal of the marketer is to create highly valuable long-term relationships with their customers, meaning: We don't want to just sell to people; we want to create mutually satisfying and beneficial relationships with them. We feed their desires and solve their problems; we are there for them when and where and how they expect, want, and need us to be. We provide value through our increased and improved ability to predict for our customers, and they provide value in terms of ROI, fanfare, and loyalty.

Wow! How?

One way to build better relationships is to service customers in ways they have come to expect. Today, both the business and the customer come to each other with a lot more transparency and data on the table, and the expectations from both sides are changing. We touched on this in the last chapter, but still, it can't be stressed enough: Customers now have more power than before. Managing your systems toward customer centricity and engagement is key.

Customer lifecycle management is a methodology, not a technology. It is used to figure out and map out the natural paths–the journey–our customers take, from the very first step of awareness all the way to termination. This approach relies on the understanding that different people take different journeys and places at the center of the map, these questions:

- How do we help people along their various journeys?

- How do we make the journey easier, so that the customer is happier and more willing to pay more money along the way?

The customer lifecycle approach entails looking at growth and success from a dynamic and complex customer perspective rather than from a one-way push model business perspective. Your message must be along these lines:

We make your life better, that's why we make our products, and that's why we want you to use them. We exist to ensure you a consistent and continuous experience across channels, over time.

The Customer Lifecycle in Action

A few of the biggest and earliest adopters of the customer lifecycle approach are banks, telecoms, cable companies, and retail. Twenty years ago, banks were eager to cut costs, so they cut back on branches and branch services. They figured they already had the customers, so why not give them something snazzy online, like E-trade. E-trade was popular, but as it turned out, people actually want their bank branch. For certain occasions, we like to have a living breathing human in front of us.

If you are a bank and you understand the customer lifecycle, you know that when somebody moves or wants to take out a loan, you should have somebody in front of them. Engage and build trust–not only because that's what they need and want, but also because this will help them buy more from you now, or down the road.

A large part of nailing down the details of your customer lifecycle involves going out–hitting the pavement, if you will–and figuring out what people expect and want. Now, if you are a very shrewd salesperson in the business of selling vacation and travel services, and people are walking into your office, what would you be looking for in their behavior that would teach you about what kind of problems you can solve?

As a human being you could do a lot, right? Yes, and now you can do a lot more online. The question is what kind of information and what kind of possibilities could you foresee that the couple that just "walked in" are looking for? Are they about to sit down and chat with you about an upcoming honeymoon, family vacation, or secret lovers' rendezvous–and what kind of information would you need to infer? This information is not going to necessarily come at you with one signal. You might get a lot of signals–some already exist, and some do not.

It costs money, of course, to attract all the necessary signals, rapidly—and then to compile, dump, analyze, and translate them. But you have to start somewhere, and you start with your map. Ask:

- What is the customer going through?

- What are our customer touchpoints?

- When are we able to touch them along the way (or, when aren't we touching them right now)?

- When and why do they get in touch with us?

- What channels can we use or create to communicate with them or meet them?

- How can we help them along this journey?

Credit card companies learned that one of their biggest lifecycle stages—a critical touchpoint—occurred when a customer's card was about to expire. Not long ago, you had to pay attention and stay on top of ordering your new card. If you didn't get your new card on time, you had to use your backup card for perhaps up to a few weeks. And then, funny thing, when that renewed card finally arrived and you had to activate it—"Seriously," you thought, "Why bother?" Your other card became your go-to card because it was there when you needed it.

One key to understanding why and how banks were losing so much money came after recognizing where the gap was and then carefully mapping out a solution. From a customer's perspective, how do we, the bank, help the customer bridge this expiration and activation stage? What solutions can we find? There were many different solutions—for any given issue, there usually are—but a simple pre-emptive action (or two) solved the problem: Send a new card before the old one expires and make activation as simple as possible. Even if it cost the banks more to do this, it was worth it.

Yes, customer journey maps can be complex—human behavior often is; but sometimes, a Psych 101 approach is all it really takes. I like to shop at Nordstrom. Over the years, they've gathered enough data on me, both in person and online, to know when my birthday is. In the old days, maybe they sent me a coupon to celebrate, but then they observed and noted and conveyed to the marketing team that I usually don't buy myself something on my birthday—that's just not what I need the most help with. What I do need help with is buying a present for my wife on her birthday—send me a coupon then, and I'm much more likely not only to use it, but to splurge some too.

Bottom line: How does a company continually work to make my life easier—to help me when I need the most help? Service providers are hardly exciting companies to deal with, but they're masters at being there for us at critical junctures—when we move, it's a breeze now to terminate the electric in one house. Then, when you arrive at your new home, a pile of coupons from all your former company's competitors is already waiting for you. Utilities lose customers at exactly this stage. So, make my move a little easier and you've won me over.

Building trust, engagement, and loyalty takes time, and it takes different amounts of time for different customers. Some will accept an upsell early on; others require a longer dance. Some want help via chat instantly; others hit "Close" as soon as the chat box appears. The question is when can we, in each of these stages, pinpoint friction and alleviate it? How can we then also delight people?

Going back to banks as an example, when they discovered that depositing checks had become a source of friction in the customer experience, they saw an opportunity to solve a problem: enter the app that allows us to deposit checks via our phones. Sure, a lot of people hate their banks—banks take our money, charge fees, and so on. But over time, if the comfort and trust apps can generate becomes associated with the brand, even banks can go from being seen as cold hard entities, to being liked! Your bank is wonderful when it solves a problem. When a company makes your life as pain-free as possible, why would you want to transfer elsewhere?

Levels of Personalization in the Customer Lifecycle

This all goes back to personalization and the notion that the more you know your customers and the more you can solve problems that are specific to them, the stickier you get.

The role of personalization in the customer lifecycle is straight-forward and simple: There are basically three levels of personalization:

1. Addressing somebody in a personal manner. Simply acknowledging the fact that you know who your customer is and what stage they're at in their relationship with you, has an impact. "Hi Caroline, thank you for being a loyal customer for the past year," shows a certain level of specificity. As this becomes standard, it won't be enough, but right now, it makes people feel good—and that's a good start.

2. Addressing someone at the right time. Rather than addressing a customer every Friday or at whatever time is convenient for you, address them at a time that makes sense to them. "We

realize you are moving, so we're sending you a discount on bedding."

3. Communicating with custom content in custom context. This is high-level personalization. You're helping solve problems. You're providing an exceptional experience. You're making your customers' lives easier, and you are promoting dependency on all of the above.

We talk a lot about subtlety in personalization, but marketers haven't traditionally been trained in the art of subtlety, have we? It's always been: I have this customer for eight weeks, somebody handed them over to me. This is my opportunity to get them to activate as many services as possible, because that's my KPI. How am I going to get them to activate? I'm going to email them every Friday for these eight weeks. Have you activated yet? Hello again, have you activated yet? Dear Kate, don't miss out on our special activation fee!

Subtle? No. Now: Let's step back and try to identify each individual. Is a weekly email for eight weeks what they need right now? What are their needs? How can we solve these needs? What happens if we're patient and build the trust for four of the eight weeks and maybe activate them later?

The customer-centric lifecycle approach recognizes that different people have different journeys. Work with them in a way that is right for them—and not necessarily your way—and your overall customer value will go up.

The Funnel, The Customer Lifecycle, and the Mesh Walk Into a Marketing Conference

The funnel is a way of logically saying, "Hey, Mr. X. I want you to do A. Then, I'm going to want you to do B. Then, I'm going to do C, which will result in you doing D. As I lead you down that path, I'm going to trap you into doing 1, 2, 3, 4 and I'm going to try to push you as fast as possible–our goal here is maximum velocity."

This is way sales and sales people think and work: How can I push them to the next meeting? How can I get them to commit to letter of intent? How can I get a quote to them? How can I get them to respond? How do I route them to someone who can sell to them as quickly as possible?

The funnel approach requires pushing as aggressively as possible to bring your customers to a decision point, by having them make smaller and smaller decisions. Anybody who leaks out of the funnel is seen as "proof" that marketing and sales failed to convert, failed to move them to the next step, or failed in the overall funnel-building process. The entire focus then reverts to trying to bring "the lost" back into the funnel.

In customer lifecycle management, funnels are not gone completely, but are used as a tactical approach to a specific touch-point (usually in the acquisition stage).

One of the ideas of the funnel is that we control the environment in which we deal with the customer or prospect. They come to our website and we manipulate and control what direction the encounter will take on that website, until they leave it. It's not that simple anymore. In many cases, there are many different places a customer might meet us: website, mobile site, mobile app, and so on. They come to us via tablet, laptop, home desktop, work desktop, public desktop, and so on. There is also TV, in-store, on the street, or at a kiosk. What a huge pile of spaghetti—and let's not forget to add the virtual assistants and virtual reality stuff that's coming into play.

Losing control over the user interface—losing control over the number of different channels, devices, and touch points—has up until very recently, been considered problematic: "Oh no! We can't control the message we're providing. We can't control the when, where, and to whom. We're doomed!"

But if we view this huge constantly flashing tangle from a different angle, we can see it as a mesh that is similar to the force in Star Wars! It is all around us; it binds us together; and it is power. Dear Customers: The mesh is customer-centered, because all of your devices know you. They track you and therefore give you, as a user, power. This of course gives brands power too—and the best brands use their power for good: they use their power to help you when and where you most need it!

Marketers who think the mesh is a headache will stay stuck. Those who figure it out will be gold. Customers will adopt and identify themselves in the mesh. Once they do, they'll be locked in forever. Information is passed on and spread out and you have opportunities to know customers you had no access to before. But of course, you have to be creative. Data alone is just data. Consider the customer journey: Consider why they invested in a house that adjusts temperature and sound for them, and a car that knows the three fastest ways to their office and favorite restaurants, depending on traffic.

We have the potential to know what's going on thanks to all this data that is being poured and pulled into the system. The fact is, not only is there an opportunity for us as a brand to hook in and service customers better, but their expectations are also being refined and elevated. They expect us to better their lives, and we must keep up. Bottom line: Very soon, if not already now, you should be communicating and interacting with your customers based on the context of the data they share, that is, what do certain major and minor events mean to them, right now?

Again, let's look at Nike: If they were to send their communications through the most traditional marketing route, then they would simply email their customers at exactly the point where the average shoe lifecycle is ending. Instead, they do better: Every time somebody is running, Nike is calculating how many miles they've run (through their app), and wait for the X-miles mark to suggest a new pair. Good, but no longer good enough. So of course, Nike goes for deeper more meaningful signals: Is this runner preparing for a marathon this year? Do they want better shoes? Are they running slower than they were running before? What surface do they tend to run on? What's happening with this runner, this year or this month, as compared to a year or two ago?

How can marketers find signals? How can we analyze signals to determine accurate context and help our customers solve problems? Perhaps we can create experiences that will teach us more about context, for example, we can build an app that doesn't provide what we're selling, but provides data of some other kind that helps us know our customers and solve their problems.

Uber does what, primarily? It gets us around. What if Company X wanted to know where all 21-25 year olds were going in Portland, Oregon right now–which clubs were hot? What if they partnered with Uber–created an app, shared data?

Uber and American Express are sharing data right now. Uber takes somebody somewhere, and American Express knows what was purchased. These companies are working together to anticipate and predict behavior, and to make more timely and relevant suggestions and offers. Think about it: If somebody just needs Uber to get some place, why not call a cab? Because Uber is showing that it is trying to solve bigger challenges than just "getting people there." They are truly "going the extra mile."

In fact, Uber has an API, so you can connect with them and bring that data into your own mesh. This API offers Uber passengers unique content and experiences based on what kind of trip they are taking: The five-minute commuter gets five minutes of news; the visiting weekend warrior gets hot Happy Hour deals; and the woman returning home after dark can turn her exterior lights on before she steps out of the vehicle. Of course, currently, some of this technology is only highly relevant to travel-related apps–but the possibilities for going the extra mile in other industries is exciting.

*

Invest in data and in teams that have the intelligence and insight to put it all into context, and you'll have access to what is happening right now with your customers. From there, you can design customer communication and experiences that allow you to keep showing up at the places your customers frequent–with the solutions they are seeking. Do this more often, and the more people will feel comfortable with you; the more they feel comfortable with you, the more they need you. The customer lifecycle is fast, but at times patient; it is widespread and everywhere, but intimate; it is as solid and dependable as mom and pop, but as agile and ambient as the mesh.

Chapter Five

Where We Find Personalization

E-commerce: Obviously

E-commerce is all about getting people as close as possible to the cause of any given interaction, and is probably the most obvious place where personalization can provide high returns for the vendor. Typically, it focuses around product recommendations and "inspired by your wishlist" communications, but it may also include tactics such as a subscription feature, where customers receive discounts on refills of frequently purchased products such as razor blades and diapers.

Using the subscription tactic may not be the deepest form of personalization, but it is a way of anticipating what customers will need, and saving them the time of even having to realize they need it. "You need to replace your vacuum cleaner bags" helps ensure a customer won't get "caught" midway through cleaning their house for the big family reunion bash, and have to stop and run out to the local store to finish the job.

E-commerce personalization, therefore, can look more or less "traditional," but it is located everywhere throughout the digital experience and it pulls in as much data as possible. Customers then receive personalized messaging or content in any or all of the following forms:

- Recommendations for you based on your recent choices, or browsing history, or what you've left in your cart.

- Recommendations based on people that are similar to you.

- What to buy next, i.e. add-ons-"Here's another product that will go well with the one you purchased last week."

- Coupons in emails and newsletters.

- Drop-down menus: If I'm a man browsing REI's men's fashion, the drop-down menu for men is presented to me before the drop-down menu for women.

- Search results: Google is, of course, the pioneer here, altering the order of an individual's search results based on his or her browsing history, etc.

Content: Out of the Potential Patchwork of Pieces

Some marketers say that content is too unwieldy to personalize, but I've found that it's not impossible. On blogs, you can put together a compelling variety of stories, and on content hubs, you can put together a wide range of engaging content–such as blog-like stories, customer service Q & A's, case studies, "how to" articles, and so on.

The order in which the content is organized does not have to be the same for every visitor. If we are in the business of making airplane engines (in addition to several other types of engines), and we know that you are the airplane engine buyer for Air France and need to retrofit some of your planes, we will do all we can to stand out in the "airplane engine manufacturer" category in the particular content hubs we expect you to frequent.

We can do the same with images and location. Of course, this is frequently done with advertisements: We send out images of men in rugged outdoor gear or in pencil jeans and graphic tees if we know a young male individual in the Pacific Northwest is reading a fashion article–and we know if he buys kayaks and headlamps, or triple non-fat skinny mochaccinos and bags of loose tobacco.

We can go deeper with content personalization by utilizing all kinds of interactive pieces of content, such as surveys. For instance, we ask a question or a series of questions, and based on the answer(s) provided, we change–in real time–some of the content we are about to send out.

If we commit to always and forever measuring the analytics, we can run different versions of tools as seemingly complex and static as e-books. In the banking industry, for example, the mid-level executive and the COO both click for our free e-book today, but the book each receives is slightly different, because we know their job title before we fulfill their order.

We also know before we present content and take action, what stage of the customer lifecycle a person is at. If they are just exploring what we do and what we offer, we don't necessarily want to show them pricing plans or competitor comparisons. We simply want to show them our cool stuff!

Adobe, for instance, offers first time and newbie visitors to their homepage a free 30-day trial. When you revisit this "same" homepage a couple weeks into your trial however, the page changes and prompts: "Are you ready to buy now?" The brand makes upgrading and finalizing that first key purchase not only 100% accessible, but seamless. Adobe knows that right now, you stepping closer to them instead of away from them, is all that matters in the world.

Interactive content, such as mortgage or "find out what CMOs like you are making" calculators, is the newest field, and it strives to do two things:

- Provide a more engaging and memorable experience.
- Obtain more information about the prospect or about the customer.

The hottest thing now with interactive content is happening with apps, where personalized user interfaces are being built.

Advertising and Retargeting: Know When to Hold 'Em, Know When to Fold 'Em

Contrary to the cutting edge highly tailored interactive personalization techniques in the world of apps, we've got our old-school advertising and retargeting efforts. Personalization may be somewhat less "exciting" here—and probably has less potential—but again, just because we have big data, high tech, and the mesh, does not mean we have to throw the baby out with the bathwater.

With ads, you can't get too personal (i.e. you can't show personal data like their name) but you can pick an ad out of your inventory to match to the customer based on page visit or lifecycle stage.

You have probably seen retargeting in action: When you browse a travel website and search for a hotel in Rome, for the next twenty-four hours or so, you see ads everywhere you go on the web for cheap hotels in Rome. You see coupons and discounts for rooms in Rome. What's happening here is if this travel site is using a text ad, they can dynamically populate the text field with snippets of Roman history or customs. If they have a visual ad, they can utilize a bank of Rome images. This "basic" level of personalization–targeting–borders on segmentation: it says, "Somebody visited the specific page X that includes tag Y, so show them ad Z." But targeting aims to get us closer to a personalized experience, and is highly effective when delivered at the right stage of the customer lifecycle.

Email: Let's Up This Game

Email is still a main channel and a lot of marketers do a lot with it. Email, of course, can range from the generic "Hi, Daniel" level of personalization we've addressed in previous chapters, to a much more refined and sophisticated communication tool: "Hi, Daniel. Because you are an author of a book about personalization, we just thought this would be interesting."

From there, everything else in the body of the message might be generic–but again, it's how that first chord strikes us that matters most. It is the promise of a company knowing us that lures us closer, that makes us read, research, share information, and perhaps, convert.

With email now, some marketers are getting more personal: "Do we really know who Daniel is, and if so, how can we create a fresh and dynamic experience for him?"

If a company's marketing emails or newsletters consist of some mix of generic content, original content, and one article from their blog, how can they ensure I haven't already visited their blog and read that very same article? "Hmm," I say upon opening that "highly personalized" email, "But I already read that post. Yes, time to unsubscribe. Too much information; too much clutter; not enough VIP!"

We've addressed the VIP effect—the notion that you can create experiences that make customers at all levels and touch points feel special. Some of these VIP tools require heavier spending than others, but here's a really cool trick almost anyone can do: Studies show that people like people with similar names. Jane Walsh doesn't know why, but she has a tiny sense of affinity when the cable company CSR emailing her is named Jake Walls. It's subconscious: "Hmm," Jane thinks, "I better give this email some attention."

This similar-sounding-name trick is usually a simple one to pull off, and you could go on forever in email, but where marketers fail the most with email is with timing. Timing is very personal, and sending emails out based on "averages" (i.e. ten days after sign up), now strikes many customers as "off" or off putting. When does Daniel want to see emails—every week or every two weeks? Sometimes you can determine this algorithmically, sometimes you should just ask: Dear Daniel, do you want to see product notifications? Do you want a digest of articles weekly or full links daily? Is there a best time of day for you to receive your requested emails?

In-Store: The Struggle is Real, but Manageable

In-store expenditures are interesting because they are beginning to happen in tandem with apps and cutting edge technology, i.e. QR codes and pop up and/or push notifications. These online-offline mixes constitute cutting edge blended experiences, and are so new, not many marketers have a good grip on them just yet.

But other very simple acts of personalization take place in-store now too: you notice that more salespeople thank you by name for shopping with them. They are doing so because your name appears when you pass your credit card through their system. It's digital, and it's a very subtle touch, but in-store personalization has to make the most of every tidbit of information available, especially if they are not a Mom and Pop store where they do actually know you by name.

A main goal of personalization in-store is obviously to create an engaging and compelling experience. But on top of that–and here is the added modern-day pressure–staff has to do whatever it takes to make sure that in-store customers do not get on Amazon while in-store, to compare prices (and to hit Buy on the spot).

Big name brick and mortars have been struggling with this "showroom for Amazon" phenomenon for years now, and some have folded, but those who make it, do so by providing customers with an excellent personal experience, where they feel like they're being taken care of and are just too happy to bother comparing prices with Amazon.

The Body Shop, for example, can provide an experience Amazon can't (at least not until someone invents the technology to deliver smell over the Internet). Even if you don't sell soap and cream, there are plenty of ways to provide unique customer experiences: Ralph Lauren recently installed an interactive fitting room in their Fifth Avenue store. Other retailers are using their buyers' personal data to reorganize their store layout and effectively manage inventory (i.e. making sure that loyal customers always have their sizes in stock). Companies are also using beacon technologies to customize their app's functionality. For example, if the customer's location is "in store" or on site, it's a no-brainer: If a customer is already in the store, they don't need the store-locator feature.

Stores, like real live teachers and actual books made of paper, will never go away–despite all the early "threats" that technology and online experiences would render them obsolete. Everything is adapting and evolving–and thus, improving.

Mobile Apps: The Sky's the Limit

You can do almost anything with mobile apps, from the obvious, i.e. gaining access to your bank account and being able to perform actions like depositing a check, or checking in for a flight. If an airline knows that your flight is running late and is overbooked, they should send you a personal notification and maybe recommend some hotels nearby.

Apps beat websites for personalization in a couple ways:

- They run natively, so they're faster.
- You can design them to do anything.
- They have access to a customer's essential data via their phone (i.e. a mobile app can tell you how many flights of stairs the

person has climbed today, where and at what altitude, and at what time.)

Apps can provide app developers and brands with tremendous amounts of valuable data. Sometimes, there is actually way too much data–what are you going to do with a person's altitude, for example, unless you are some sort of mountaineering or sports company? Maybe you've got a recipe app, and altitude counts for cooking temperature adjustments, but either way, the point is, some information is useful and usable, some is not. Design your app according to what material you want most to mine.

The Starbucks' app knows your drink preferences, and is the Number One brick and mortar with an app (talk about an excellent blended experience). Bank apps rank high–how much easier is it now to transfer money to your kid at college than it was just five years ago? REI has an app that helps you find nearby hiking trails. The Six Flags and Disney apps, though perhaps not as well-used as Starbucks, pack powerful personalized blended experiences.

All of these apps, of course, capture customer data and create new touch points with the brand, which in turn, can lead to a mutual exchange of more precise and relevant content. Customers don't always realize (yet), that the data a company is using for personalizing email is coming from the app.

The challenge with apps is that it can be extremely difficult to get people to download and activate them, and equally as challenging to then pull people back to use them repeatedly. Very few brands have managed to continuously engage a sizable proportion of their customers on their app(s).

Education: Lessons for Us All

At first glance, education may appear to be outside the scope of this book, but in my mind, personalization in education is a highly interesting field that marketers can learn from. Our children are experiencing a new wave in personalized education: While many educators and parents have always known that people don't learn things in the same way and at the same pace, technology is finally available that supports teachers, parents, and students in ways we previously only dreamt of.

Education can be adjusted and tailor made: Some people are highly visual, others are auditory–some want to watch a how-to video, while others prefer to read text. Even the type of assessments students are given can now be adapted. Now, rather than viewing individuals as having "special needs," we recognize that basically, what we all have are "needs."

Personalized education systems adapt to the learner's preferred learning style and provide further enhancements. You see this with learning games, such as Math Dragon, which rather than simply reporting the number of errors students make along the way, then gives them more exercises of the type they're having trouble with, until they can master it. Student progression through a course is not necessarily an A to Z path, and is not always at the same pace as others. There is a dialogue, a technologically-based dialogue, throughout, and it is this back and forth process that most resembles what marketers and brands can do with their customers: How are we moving our customers along the customer lifecycle–how are we helping them? How are we "training" them to make better and faster decisions in terms of buying our product or service, and succeeding with us? Most importantly, how are we making our customers happy?

Many of us in marketing believe we are getting better at setting our systems up so that we get the data and feedback we need, which we can then turn into incentives for our customers. This person is a walker and this person is a runner–the runner is moving faster over more territory, so we'll get that shoe offer to her sooner. But in the end, we want both customers to cross the finish line, that is, to need new shoes.

To keep improving personalization in marketing, we should definitely look to personalization in education, where there is already an understanding that giving students the freedom not just to learn at their own pace, but to learn what it is they most want to learn–is key to success and therefore, to fulfillment and happiness. Okay, in school, certainly, at the end of the year you have to meet certain benchmarks, but hey, John Doe, if you want to study more algebra right now because that's what you're into and you want to take on geometry later in the year, that'll work.

In the old days, students who were ahead or behind created disruption for the entire class–teachers were overworked and didn't know how to control them. Now, the system is catching up. What if we look at customers in the same light? Each has his or her own journey: If this customer wants to go faster and we could easily onboard her for only two weeks instead of eight, let's hustle! Why keep everybody onboard for eight weeks simply because that's the way we've always done it–that's the way we've divided our business between departments?

If you want to see where personalization is going, take a look at cutting edge education technologies. If you want to take a bold leap ahead of the competition, put your resources into marketing technologies that take into account "differences in (learning) styles. The generations that are currently growing up with a "succeed at your own pace, with your unique menu, preferences, and style," are graduating from high school and college–they are going to become your customers and they're going to say, "Why can't I have all the adult things the way I've been educated and trained to expect them? If you don't deliver personalized shopping experiences to these new generations of personalized schooling experiences, prepare to hear lots of voices on social media declaring: "You suck," because like it or not, that's the jargon.

Chapter Six

Managing with an Eye Toward Personalization

Considering the pace marketing departments must maintain today and the rate of change and expansion we are going through, it's hard to nail down a definition of the ideal CMO–it's hard to say precisely what qualities any of us CMOs should embody. There are however, three top keys to managing with personalization in mind:

- Technology: As it continues to move out of the IT department, into the marketing department, and across all departments-to varying degrees.

- Analytics: Setting up and reviewing all the systems, data, and insight technology can bring us, through a customer journey lens.

- Legal: Beyond the basic legal considerations all businesses must take into consideration, because we are relying more on more on collecting much more personal and confidential material, marketers must think about consequences. We must think about the customer's security and well-being.

Legal is a topic I haven't touched on yet, and its significance will become even more evident in Chapter Seven, where I discuss the future of marketing. But for now, let's briefly look at the Pokemon Go phenomenon. This former "game only," is currently being presented by Nintendo marketers, in part, as a health and well-being app. They're claiming it encourages people to step outside and be more active, and it probably does push some of its players toward a healthier lifestyle. But at the same time, stories of the app causing car accidents and being used to commit crimes are already circulating; and how active or social is a game where everyone is wandering around mostly with their necks craned to their devices and their eyes glued to wherever the Pokemon are lurking? I'm not judging Pokemon Go one way or another, and don't know exactly how the game is played—the point is: How does legal begin to tackle the pros and cons and nuances of such products? Clearly, we are diving into legal realms we've never previously encountered, which is endlessly intriguing, and a challenge marketers have to stay on top of.

Technology, analytics, and legal, of course, are not the only considerations to take into account when managing with an eye toward personalization—and these elements may shift according to project specifications and goals—but ultimately a CMO wants to always be asking his or her team: "Given X, Y, and Z, what could we do to ramp up our personalization efforts here?"

Then, after we pursue and test several coulds, we determine what's feasible.

The fact is, we know all about the personalization hype, but many organizations, brands, and services still are not applying what they know as well as they could be, and are therefore not benefitting from its full effects.

We know there is this basic level of personalization that says, "Great! I have the technology and am capable of adding a person's name to an email." But at this stage of the game, we know this is not full personalization—and our customers know too. Full personalization entails giving each and every customer the feeling that they have an intimate and unique relationship with the brand. It means helping them when they need help, and when they don't know they need it. It also means getting to know them more, in order to find more opportunities to help.

Obviously, we've been marketing for decades, but we haven't been thinking about personalization in light of the technology we have today for very long at all—and most of us admit, no matter what generation we're a part of, that wrapping our brains around the endless possibilities can be overwhelming. We also have come to realize that though we have more data than ever, not all of it is the right data—or, not all of it is relevant to all of our projects. And in spite of all the data we have and are already sorting through and managing, there are countless things we still do not know about our customers that we wish we did.

For example, say a credit card company is thinking of new and improved ways to service their customer, John Smith. "Ah-ha!" they say. "Let's try providing him with travel insurance." Great idea, but how do they know that John is planning on traveling in the first place? They need to have the tools in place to access all the signals this particular customer might be sending that might indicate he is thinking about going to Disneyland France, because if John Smith is already in France and hasn't bought his travel insurance, they have already lost. Credit card marketers looking to personalize need to ask, "How can we learn in advance that our customers are planning to travel–what kind of travel is this, and with whom?"

Managing with an eye toward personalization in this case means finding a creative way to ask your customers, "Are you planning a trip?" Managing with an eye toward personalization means I can ask my tech guy to sort through all of the purchases my customers are making and to produce an algorithm that shows me what kind of purchasing patterns indicate "possible future trip," so that even when we don't know with 100% confidence what our customers are up to, we have a mechanism set in place that subtly and creatively says: "We think you're planning a trip. Are you?" Once that set of travel-ready customers answers, "Yes," we can really flood them with the right messages, helping them with their trip and helping us with our profits.

There are many similar lifecycle moments, or what we call meaningful moments. John Smith is planning a trip and needs a rental car plus travelers' insurance; Paulo Ruiz is planning another child, which means he might be buying a newer safer car; somebody is starting to think about college savings plans; and somebody else is about to retire. These meaningful moments are not always trigger-based, that is, they are not necessarily moments that marketers pick up on when somebody visits a website and gives us a very obvious signal by clicking a button. But by asking what we could do, we marketers will find ways to work around what is less-than-obvious–we will find the technology to do so.

T to + and Crushing Silos

In marketing, traditionally the key profile for our employees has resembled the letter "T," where the x-axis–which represents areas of expertise–sits high on the y-axis. That is to say, up until fairly recently, marketers were expected to know a lot about one vertical element or specialty, but not to deeply know much outside their wheelhouse. Today though, when it comes to managing with an eye toward personalization and developing a strong marketing team in that vein, the connection between technology, analytics, creative, and management is much tighter. Our "T" resembles more of a "+", because everyone on the marketing team has to have a hands on, deep understanding in many fields. Yes, I've said it before and I'll say it again: Dear CMO, No matter how politically challenging it is, you are going to have to crush silos.

Say you're a cell phone service provider and you acquire several surveys showing that ten-year old kids are now getting cell phones and data plans. You ask: "How can we reach our customers who have kids between the ages of eight and twelve? What kind of promotion can we offer to get more cell phones to more kids?"

The problem is, you aren't sure which of your customers have kids and which don't, so you need to figure out a way to get that information, and then how to get it from different departments: CRM, email, creative, legal, and so on. This means bringing all these departments together, along with all department managers–which means, bottom line, facing all kinds of objections. You know why you should do it this way, but the guy in the other silo knows why you shouldn't. Someone will be afraid that if they budge, either something will be taken away or more work will be dumped on them. As CMOs, it is our job to have the depth of knowledge to be able to say, "No, guess what: This is possible and we're going for it."

As marketers, the first departments we're likely to butt heads with are the IT or CRM departments. Anybody in charge of a vital system will be the first to try to keep things under their own control, so we have two approaches:

1. Bring them onboard very early, while still in talks with vendors. Bringing other departments into the planning phase ensures they are on the same page as us, in terms of what the problems and solutions are. Pre-onboarding, try to identify where the usual suspects who might say no later are residing and never assume other departments are going to approve your latest and greatest new material.

2. Plan budgets for your own technology, so that when necessary, you can go around unruly or uncooperative departments. I've seen this trend a lot, where managers buy new software to gain independence from another department, (oftentimes, the IT department).

Problems with other departments aren't the only obstacle CMOs face. If you are a powerful visionary, you'll often simply be moving way too fast for your team, or way too fast for them to understand what your vision is and how it benefits the company, the department, or the individual employees. Remember that deep down, we are all creatures of habit and comfort—many people balk at change and fear it will mean doing more for less, or again, losing something they have held dear or reliable. If your team doesn't understand why they've been asked to shift gears or direction, there will be friction and possible attempts at sabotage.

There are two ways to quell the doubt that invariably arises, particularly on big projects, which are very visionary in nature, and especially with established teams that have been part of a company for some time:

1. During the planning phase, do the extra work of trying to walk them through what the goals are and how the team will achieve them. Have regular progress meetings to review keys ideas and to keep everyone fully engaged. Never hit your team out of the blue with The Next Amazing Big Project.

2. Identify which individuals on your team or other teams A) do not quite understand what the benefits of a project or plan are, and B) are uncertain how their own future will be affected. Then, sit with them and work these issues through.

When bringing someone new in—a personalization specialist or an analyst—obviously you expect them to understand how systems fit together. A successful personalization specialist will work slightly like a politician and a product manager, in that she or he will have to run between departments that they don't have direct control over, and get them to work together. These specialists are key stakeholders, but ultimately they are not the boss, and have to accept that fact. Their role is to understand personalization as it relates to your (the CMO's) vision, and to then be very good at coordinating people and "translating" all of the tools and materials each team needs to understand in order to move forward.

Analysts, on the other hand, are a whole different breed. You find data people who can sit for days uncovering or discovering patterns. When we want to figure out which of our customers are "more into entertainment," for example, we might take a proactive approach and buy data from a company like Uber, which might show us a new segment of "people who go to certain kinds of dance clubs on weeknights."

The other approach utilizes already existent data. We ask our analysts to look through data and find new segments that maybe we haven't thought of before? For example, maybe we've only ever thought of Uber users as nightlife-seekers or young people on the go, but what if people with kids also use the service? Where do these families go and what do they do? What can we learn here, and then how can we proactively reach out?

No matter who is on my team or who I bring in, the key qualities everyone must bring to the table are curiosity and keen observation skills. Beyond understanding marketing, I want people who, when they get a piece of data, start asking: "How can we help these people and what can we sell them?" Beyond this question, I want people who can see patterns, not just in the numbers, but in the real world. My young daughter said to me recently: "People with tattoos smoke." This kind of fresh-eyed and perceptive way of viewing people is crucial in marketing, and must take place inside the office and out.

Are Your Personalization Efforts Working?

How do we measure the effects of our personalization efforts and how do we prove them? This will vary between one company and another, and we've already discussed how personalization impacts a company's KPI. We know that companies that provide excellent personalized experiences see KPI uplift. The question is: What is your goal in each personalization project, and for each sub-department, how do you translate that goal?

If you don't have a baseline, establish one. Then measure how each department is contributing to the KPI.

Say you have an unfolding program, like Direct TV, and are losing customers because they are signing up for a service, but not activating it at. If they aren't activating, they could cancel. There is unfolding churn: They aren't connecting the box, for whatever reason, and in the meantime, they get another offer that is 50% cheaper than yours and take it.

Different departments will be involved in this personalization project–the question is: What is each department's KPI target for the project? If we want to reduce the churn rate, is the marketing department responsible? The IT department? How? What is the personal incentive for each department? What is each department's role and what actions do they need to take in relation to the KPI? It's basic Management 101, but many companies don't work that way. Assigning roles and boundaries early on will help the project succeed better.

Build into the planning phase the ability to measure effects. I often work on projects at large enterprises, and often see teams of people become excited about a project, approve it, and then assume what the outcome or effects of the project will be. Unfortunately, only after the project has started do they realize: "Wait, how are we going to actually measure KPI impact?"

Looking at aftereffects is much harder and slows down a project. Not taking the necessary time to think things through–or to apply patience and logic in the "honeymoon phase," is common because:

- In the initial phases of a project, everyone is busy getting corporate and stakeholder buy-in, focusing solely on persuading people to sign off. "If I show them that's it's a little more complex than what they're thinking, they might kill the project. I don't want to scare them, so for now, I won't bother with talk of measurement."

- People assume that measuring is easy. "We'll just go for it, and later we'll ask the BI people to measure the impact."

For example, a car company might hold events in its showroom and say, "Ooh and ahh, that event was wonderful." But if the goal of the project–the KPI–was to increase the number of test drives people take in the weeks following, you have to build into the project the ability to identify the people who came to the event and eventually took a car out for a spin, which means you might have to cross-over data from two departments, and those systems might not be compatible.

At the start of every project, ask: "How are we going to connect the pieces and measure them?" If the measuring is taking place in a different department, there is no guarantee that department is going to be willing to cooperate or share their findings because perhaps they won't want to allocate their resources to what they see as someone else's baby. Generally, it's best to make no assumptions.

Obsession

CMO's are mostly obsessed with the big picture and how to build brand reputation, brand awareness, the brand experience, and the customer experience. We are not concerned with how to get the CRM people to think a little bit differently, or what customer data goes into the CRM. The opportunities to build your brand via personalization are tremendous, and CMOs want to always be in a place where they can ask themselves questions about trends. CMOs want to be curious, aware, and forward-thinking. People, at the time this book went online anyway, are going wild about Pokemon Go—so, is it here to stay? Is Pokemon Go relevant to our customers? How does or doesn't its relevancy or irrelevancy effect our customers' perception of our brand–whatever it may be–and their behaviors and relationship to us?

Is Nike going to encourage people to run after Pokemon Go? Are some restaurants going to figure out a way to learn enough about their customers to know which are Pokemon Go players, and perhaps which rare Pokemons these specific player customers have yet to collect? Whatever your business, if some of your customers are obsessed with Pokemons, you can make a decision: "Do I want to do something about it? Do I want to create experiences around Pokemon?" Some businesses are definitely already doing it: Yelp, for example, added a Pokemon filter to their search criteria.

The point is, whether we are talking about an interactive real-time video game full of cute yellow creatures, or the most sensible software on the planet, this is what the future of personalization is beginning to look like–the future has indeed already begun.

Chapter Seven

The Future of Personalization

Most games are inherently personalized. Designed to ensure each player will stick around, they are not so difficult that they discourage, nor so easy that they are boring. As CMO, I ask myself: "Can I approach my customers' lives in a similar way: Can I engage them by being interesting enough–and necessary–and yet, not so completely obtainable that they won't value the service?"

Gamers of all kinds have understood this hook for a long time. At casinos, for example, cameras track your every move. If they see that you haven't been winning, after a while they might send someone over to you–seemingly randomly–to say "Congratulations! You've won two tickets to tonight's David Copperfield show." Sure, you just lost a tremendous amount of money, but the industry wants to make sure you keep feeling like a winner.

And sure, some might say the casino industry is a nasty one that takes advantage of the lonely and addicted, but isn't that really what we marketers all dream of: That we'll attract customers who will become addicted to our services? And all that will be required of us is that we make sure they stay addicted by tweaking their journey a little bit–by giving them something a tad personal or slightly different?

We do have the tools and systems now, to grab customers and keep them coming back for more; we are learning to use these tools and systems more effectively and efficiently on a daily basis. And as if the current state of marketing weren't exciting enough, there are all sorts of intriguing and even mind-blowing trends on the horizon.

Now Trending

One very interesting, just-budding trend in personalization involves connecting what we know about the end user–the data–to the manufacturing process. Essentially, you and I could both order the same product from the same factory, but you would get something slightly different than I would, based on your needs. Say you are gluten intolerant, and I'm not: We can order the very same breakfast cereal, Oat Circles for CMOs, and this company could use the same exact manufacturing process to create slightly different products.

This just-in-time manufacturing is not currently widespread or completely doable, but it is highly personalized and promises to result in a whole different level of efficiency. Product returns with this kind of system will be lower; and satisfaction, loyalty, and profits higher. Most interesting, perhaps, is that the entire notion of a brand will change, so that what a brand represents to you might be different than what the very same brand represents to me.

Marketers, let that sink in for a minute–a single brand will assume a whole different level of complexity.

When this new form of personalized manufacturing and branding does more fully kick in, there will be production chain implications. Think about how this will look in a variety of industries: automobiles, furniture, and food (i.e. the company that makes Oat Circles for CMOs has "gluten free" written on more of their packages in Oregon than in Texas). Or, while we're on breakfast, think coffee! If you demand fair traded Morning Pickup coffee beans and I simply go for Morning Pickup's taste, soon, Morning Pickup will have the same production line for fair traded and for just plain "deliciously old-fashioned" coffee; but, different beans will be poured into the system, tracked, and packaged–in a way that is personalized. Even if the coffee were identical, the benefits on the package could be presented differently. Personalized packaging, how cool is that!

The mesh of data that surrounds you now and is helping marketers further hone in on your tastes in movies, books, clothes, cars, sofa upholstery, and consumables, will eventually interact with a mesh that is being built up around the manufacturing process. There will be practical implications, to be sure, but what those will be exactly, we don't know yet. In an ideal marketer's world, because we know more about you, we also know a lot about your friends–already, most consumers are connecting their social media channels more and more to various service providers and brands. This is convenient, and people don't really notice they're doing it anymore, but they are. As these fields of data become vaster and more accurate, another real question in marketing becomes: Do we personalize the message based on the person, or do we personalize the message based on the person's network? This kind of thinking and strategizing requires a whole different level of complexity that we aren't even close to mastering yet–but we'll get there.

The point is that maybe the next big thing after personal personalization will be personal network personalization. The point is also: Who really knows what the next big thing will be and who knows what we will be able to know even just twelve months from now?

Think about what we used to know about our customers and what we know today. We are already surrounding ourselves with these nebulous but growing meshes of data–Siri knows where we are and who we're talking to and our home monitoring systems knows who's at home, and who isn't. Everything is being tracked, and this is not only acceptable, but expected.

Customers expect to be tracked, and they expect a mutually gratifying and mutually valuable return on that "sharing." For example, Trip Advisor might see I'm in New York City, but if it suggests I check out the local bars and I'm on a family trip, I'll be annoyed: "What the heck? Trip Advisor doesn't understand me." Their job is to help me have the best trip possible–under a variety of circumstances–and this is the reason I provide all the personal information I do. I filled out some form at some point, the system is learning me, and when the system gets it right, I feel very comfortable with it, even if I don't remember what I told them, what I didn't tell them, or what they should and shouldn't know. I will feel deeply betrayed if Trip Advisor doesn't get the difference between a trip to New York City with my family and a trip to New York City for business.

In fact, as personalization campaigns become more refined, customers will become more emotional about their brands. If I've allowed a company to "know me," if I've begun a relationship with them and they mess up, I may feel something beyond betrayal and might not only abandon them—but might hate them (and spread the word). This deeper emotional response to brands, for good and for bad, is something we don't yet fully know how to handle, but it is already starting to happen. As brands and consumers begin to develop tighter relationships with more expectations, lawsuits will become more common. If Trip Advisor, for example, sends a Top Ten Dive Bar list to a recovering alcoholic, whether or not that person somehow "told" Trip Advisor they do not drink, their expectation is still: "All my brands should know me by now." McDonald's infamously went to court over its hot coffee—imagine the first Pokemon Go court case, or the first "My app urged me to binge on a dozen cheap margaritas and I lost my job, my wife, my home" drama.

Personalized manufacturing and mass customization are full of possibilities. Imagine in medicine, where you and I take the same medication for migraines, but somehow the manufacturer is smart enough to know that I absorb each milligram at a faster rate than you do, and the dosage is tweaked based on that information. I'm no doctor, and this may be easier with patches than with pills, but still— the possibilities for custom tailoring the minutia of our lives as well as the big-ticket items and services are endless. Home security systems like Electra—as part of the mesh—may one day know everything.

For now, you have your custom food, custom cosmetics, custom razor blades—how truly custom these items are doesn't really matter from a marketer's perspective: What matters from a marketer's perspective is that each customer thinks that the product or service they're receiving is custom.

Imagine Alexa (Amazon's voice controlled home app) greeting Susan at the right moment: "Hey Susan, your personal sensors indicate that you should be ordering laundry detergent refills now, right? I placed some in your shopping cart for you. Would you like me to finalize the order?"

Susan is going to be running out of laundry detergent soon, and whether or not this is deep personalization in action or not, it doesn't matter. The marketer will be thinking: Great, but now how do I get Susan to buy a little more of this stuff? How do I proactively make it easier for her to order more? Yeah yeah yeah, place the order, Susan. I didn't even say anything about cost. You'll pay it, simply because you've signed up and on for this service, and it is so convenient that you hardly take note of the exchange.

What will become easier from a marketing standpoint is that we really don't have to convince Susan to make the purchase: We know she's running low on XYZ, we put XYZ in her cart. We know she can say "yes" or "no," but we also rely on the fact that if she says no, then she'll likely forget to go to the store to buy more product, she'll run out of the stuff, and she'll recognize the value of having us automatically do the work for her.

With this level of convenience and personalization, the risk that Susan will take the time to shop elsewhere is diminished drastically. The beauty of audio controlled voice assistance is that it's really hard for the customer to veer off to start making price comparisons.

People don't consider asking Alexa if they could find a cheaper price somewhere else, because Alexa works for Amazon, so asking her would be rude. Sure, Susan knows Alexa isn't a human, but it's interesting, isn't it, how when a brand is personalized really well, customers will still hold themselves to certain etiquette standards? Chew on that awhile!

As marketers, what we've got to focus on figuring out then is: Can we increase the frequency of Susan's purchases, can we get her to buy more products, and can we get her to buy them at a higher price? More and more, technology is allowing vendors to strategize toward a YES on all counts.

The Personal Business

Another trend we see happening now is the emergence of new business models, or new pricing models, based on personal data. For instance, today home security costs a fixed amount based on zip code, period. Nobody is taking into consideration, however, that some people leave their doors unlocked, or that some people have a lot of expensive stuff at home with a lot of shady characters coming in and out. Insurance companies don't currently have access to this type of finer detail, but we all know that in general, the more "safety-aware people" are subsidizing a significant proportion of the unsafe people. The same is true for health insurance, car insurance, and so on—to some degree.

What will happen in the near future, when sensors in the mesh allow insurance companies to truly get at the details of low-risk versus high-risk consumers? We're almost there in terms of thinking "What if we gather a bunch of new low-risk customers and lure them in by giving them a cheaper price than our competitor's? What if we charge home insurance not by a fixed rate, but by an actual risk factor that is determined by data gathered via cameras and/or smart security systems? What if we adjust our auto insurance rates based on the number of miles driven (which some companies are already doing)?"

By asking these questions—and answering them—someone is going to disrupt these stagnant industries. Someone is going to introduce a new personalization-fueled business model. Someone is going to make real money.

Of all the trends we see in the realm of personalization, the one that offers the most exiting potential rewards is the use of artificial intelligence—I'm a sci-fi fan, what can I say? Today, if I ask Siri a question like, "When is the next express train into Boston?" she doesn't know how to answer, nor do the other systems. Such questions require artificial intelligence, because in fact they consist of a series of smaller questions that don't necessarily follow the exact same logic and they query different databases.

Once we do bring the artificial intelligence more fully to the marketing game, we can start querying enormous sets of data about our customers and can then begin to make more startlingly accurate conclusions about them. Mark never told the system that he was gluten intolerant, but AI noticed something about him: He avoids buying gluten products, and in fact pays a premium not to buy gluten products. This type of data is out there right now, but humans can't really see it—AI will make it more visible.

AI can do so many things:

- Mine data and learn about your customers in ways a human never could.

- Understand human mind-set, mood, and context.

- React to specific situations in real-time.

- Adjust voice and tone, as well as brand's actual content, based on context.

Remember that mom-and-pop bookstore and how the man at the store knew all your reading preferences (because he bothered to ask your opinions about the books you bought)? Well, AI can do so much more. Within the next few years, brands will know everything about you, from whether you slept well last night or not, to what TV shows you binged on into the wee hours of the morning. In a short time from now, AI will be able to shift though all this data to find meaning and determine context–a task that is impossible to do with human labor, simply because of sheer-volume.

Has your customer been late to meetings lately? Are they working more than usual? Once marketers know the context of the data (rather than the data alone) they can get in front of customers with relevant solutions and they can present these solutions in the right way. Even mundane brands like Toothpaste can find ways to make themselves relevant to people's lives when they understand context: Too much money spent on dental care lately? How about trying this new toothpaste?

How about reacting to situations in real-time? AI can really make a difference here because different people go through different challenging moments of bulls*#it or bliss throughout their weeks and days.

Currently, customers receive alerts from their apps all the time, but if the majority of these alerts are not relevant to the situation, the customer learns to ignore them. Soon though, AI will make alerts or offers only in the right context, so customers will learn to trust them more, and to follow their instructions or engage. AI will be able to do anything–it will remind your customers that it's time to order an Uber only when they need it (AI knows Raoul took the train into work today and his next appointment is too far to walk to).

What about voice and tone? AI could potentially understand that the customer is looking to order flowers because a relative just died. Taking personalization to the next level means that the system will not insult or harm this customer with the regular 10% off a dozen red roses, but rather will suggest a more expensive and appropriate floral arrangement to take to the bereaved.

Think this "mood stuff" sounds like a marketer's ridiculous fantasy? Netflix CEO Reed Hastings says that soon Nexflix will be able to tell the mood of the person as they turn on the TV–and will then be able to offer them the perfect movie to watch.

How would you change the how, when, and where you communicate with your customer if you knew their exact mood at every moment?

The Human Touch

Why do we need bank branches? In the past, there weren't so many. You had to drive into town to go to your branch–and then somebody invented the ATM. "Oh!" everybody said. "That's it: Nobody's going to need bank branches any more; nobody's going to need tellers."

Putting ATMs on every corner was the wave of the future, and a predicted branch killer. But an interesting phenomenon occurred: The computer revolution allowed banks to hire cheaper staff, and to put fewer staff members in each branch. In turn, it became cheaper to run a branch, and so banks were able to open more of them. In the end, technology did not replace the human element, not in banking anyway.

Some industries clearly will utilize the mesh and AI more than others, and while I'm excited by opportunities for personalization that I can't even fathom now, I still believe that the future of personalization will not be 100% digital. The future of personalization is not just about digitizing the entire relationship with the customer and making it more efficient, it's also about getting personal with the customer when they need a human being, and enabling that interaction with human beings to be as beneficial and comfortable as possible. People want to see and talk to people.

Look at investment banks: because they place a high value on their relationship with you, when you call the call center, you don't get a simple, "Hello, happy to serve you today, what can I help you with?" No, you get a very personal conversation, "Oh, hi Daniel. How are you? Where are you calling from and what's new? Oh, you're traveling, that's great, let me see if I can get this authorized so you don't have to call in again."

Investment banks are very proactive. They have information about you and try to understand you, because they understand that ultimately people trust their money with other people, not with a computer. That is why eTrade (the world's most digital bank) is now opening up branches and has actual people call you to discuss your investments. Sure, the action that the people at eTrade take is triggered by big-data: A large money-wire has arrived and the customer has not used it yet. A computer determines to rout this event to a representative. Why? Because the computer determined that it takes a human voice, not an email, to build this particular relationship in this particular case.

Algorithms

Companies that are progressive–i.e. that are not silo'ed–are adoptive of new technologies and methodologies, but often they are smaller in terms of staff and resources, and therefore do not have the capacity to deal with running centers for innovation and testing of new technologies. These companies can make up for what they lack in size and funding however, by making certain managerial shifts. I've covered managing with an eye toward personalization already, but one common denominator I am seeing as marketing departments of all types and sizes is a move toward onboarding managers whose main purpose is to create change. In this regard, we are looking at a whole new class of companies that are digital and highly agile–they have grown very quickly and have been led by their talent.

This shift in managerial style ultimately results in swifter smaller newer players being able to ante up and oust the uber-powered dinosaurs. These new kids on the block are saying: "We don't have to innovate on manufacturing or anything else, we just have to innovate on the quality of the service we provide, and this service will be all be highly personalized."

Look at Bank of America–it's a crusty looking dinosaur. In comparison, some of the medium-sized banks have very nice apps, and they do a lot of work to make improvements in this area. Linking everything back to AI, we might ask, "Okay, yes, but at some point we will all have similar personalization capabilities, even the dinosaurs. So, what will the differences be between us and them?"

The answer: We'll have the manufacturing efficiency metrics and all the usual parameters, but eventually–right now, in fact–it all boils down to who understands the customer journey better. Who has the better algorithms!

A few decades from now, when you ask what the difference is between two phone companies, the answer will be an algorithm. From the marketer's perspective, from the marketing technology perspective, the answer will always be the algorithm.

Conclusion: Hook 'Em Humanely

A key role of every marketer today is to identify who in this world they can make fall in love with their product. Who needs you; who can you help? Who, if you had every possible resource at your disposal and all the capabilities in the world, is going to be your most insanely profitable audience?

The core of every CMOs mission is to figure out what features, technologies, and systems are needed to make that "insanely profitable audience" wake up and take action.

My job as CMO is to push the limits of rationality, to create spin on reality, and to push people to do what they wouldn't do if we weren't here. Maybe that is marketing, by definition. And maybe we take joy in it–I do. Questioning reality is part of my nature as a disruptive CMO, but it also leads me to new insights into human nature, and thus, customer behavior.

When you are trying to figure out how to better position your company, before worrying about pleasing all of your customers all of the time, ask yourself first if that is what you want. Then ask yourself what creativity is.

Get creative, and you'll figure out ways to obtain the data you need. Obtain the data you need and ask what kind of insight it offers. Pour over that insight as a team, or better yet, as cross-functional teams, and it will lead you to a deeper understanding of what features and services of brands or products customers love and adore most.

The bottom line, always: You want a product that speaks for itself. In the long game, it isn't the spin or the technology that works best– it's the human touch. If your company has an approach of maintaining innovative and helpful products, then that is your lead. Let the product do its thing, and leverage personalization tools and strategies to foster stronger happier customer relationships.

Rapid Takeaway: Creative Take Off

Now that you understand that the role of personalization in the customer lifecycle is dependent on any number of factors and parameters, how will you discuss it with your leadership team?

5 Qs Toward a Creative Personalization Upgrade:

- *Considering your customer's lifecycle, what potential touch-points are you currently missing out on?*

- *What meaningful moments and key life events are currently effecting (or may be soon effecting) your customer's relationship with your business?*

- *How could you personally engage with your customer in those meaningful moments to better service them and increase value?*

- *What kind of data will you need in order to achieve this this level of engagement?*

- *How will you collect, translate, and share the data you need?*

CMO confessions

BOOK 2

DISRUPT THAT

Why all marketers need to think
like startups do.

Warning: This Book Contains No Filler

The only thing worse than writing a book about marketing is reading one. ~ *Me*

I confess—my initial motivation for writing a book about marketing was to use it as collateral to get speaking gigs at conferences. I suspect most marketing books are like that, and that's probably why so many of them consist mostly of "filler" and "fluff."

The problem is, I don't have enough time to write three hundred pages of filler and fluff. For two years I have postponed writing this book, thinking that I would simply never have the time to write it. Eventually though, the realization came to me that just as I, the busy CMO, have no time to *write* a book, my readers will have no time to *read* one—not a lengthy one, anyway. The problem proposed the solution: Get to the point. Write a short book. Eliminate all the filler and fluff. Make it a great packed-with-punches read that someone could consume while taking the Acela train from Boston to New York. On top of it all: Deliver value by offering people a new perspective.

So, no book filler—I promise.

As I got started with the book, my initial motivation to use it as collateral faded. I realized that my experience leading marketing departments in innovative cutting-edge departments from Tel-Aviv to Boston gives me a definitively unique perspective. And because most books on marketing are written by marketing theorists, not marketing doers, I have a real chance to deliver real value. How?

By confessing that in many ways, despite all the tools and data we now have at hand—marketing remains a wildly unpredictable and unknowable "guessing" game. Or, at the very least, it relies heavily on intuition and sometimes, sheer dumb luck and a certain kind of rambling and bumbling creative approach.

Marketing is a tough industry. When I first set out to plan this book, I thought I might call it: *The CMO's Two-Year Shot,* emphasizing how quick turnaround can be at the top. A company brings you onboard, and you rock hard while you can: It's better to burn out, than fade away, right? You take risks, you fail and learn, but above all, you disrupt. Give a smart CMO five companies in ten years to disrupt. We love it. I love it!

All marketers today must think like start-ups, we must burst out of the starting gates AS IF we do only have two years MAX with any company we work for.

(I have admitted to not having all the answers and to potentially having a shelf life of twenty-four months. I am also still interested in speaking opportunities, BTW.)

So, who is this compact but mighty book for? I hope it lands in the hands of the modern marketing executive, or anyone who wants to be us or understand us. This is one of a series of short books. It includes insights, lessons, (and yes, confessions), from my years as a CMO.

That said, I think intros suck, so let's get started. As I promised— no book filler!

Chapter One

Taming the Marketing Beast

Why Agile Marketing is Your Strategic Advantage Over the Competition

In the 1950s, it might have been easy to define "the average marketer." I don't know—I wasn't there, but traditionally, the first marketers to pop out of the newly-minted MBA programs were, like *Mad Men's* Don Draper, mystical and mythical creatures who intuitively knew what people wanted.

The ad agencies quickly leveraged this perception too—because what good is an ad agency if it doesn't prophesy and profit from what the public is willing to believe? For decades, marketing wasn't a science. It wasn't a process. It was an art. Marketing was a secret that nobody on the outside could understand; it had qualities nobody could measure. It was like red wine. Sure, if we fast-forward to today we know how practically anyone who knows the difference between a pinot noir and a merlot can wax on about red wine, but for decades, to understand marketing or red wine, we had to trust connoisseurs.

The connoisseur: Now there's a job that has become obsolete.

Today, we all have the capacity to be as well informed as we want to be. Consumers are well informed, and as marketers, we had better be several steps ahead of them. But who are we, the marketers of today?

Long gone are the days of the "average" marketer, or the stereotypical non-computer savvy, touchy-feely, mystical marketing type. Research by HBR shows that a high percentage of senior marketing managers and CMOs have no education in marketing whatsoever. A lot of us come from the quantitative sciences, such as engineering. Marketers know how to measure, and this change in who is being drawn to the field of marketing is itself, measurable.

The only sure bet in the world of marketing now is that all bets are off in terms of what mix of academic and professional backgrounds you'll find when you take a peek inside a marketing department. And all bets are off in terms of what marketing departments can count on as "the one thing to master in order to rule the universe!"

Why is this? Well, because marketing is graduating from an art to a science, and as more and more of our marketing methods are becoming digital, so are the people who head marketing departments.

The magic in marketing is gone: Our activities can be measured and so can our performance.

The magic may be gone, but there is one thing we can count on: Your CEO, no matter how enlightened, empowering, and empathetic, will still consistently enter the room, drop a bomb of a deadline, and turn to you, the head of the marketing department, and expect magic.

We do perform magic, but today we do so less by sleight of hand than by swiftness of process. The magic we need to master today lies in our ability to achieve more with fewer resources. The marketing department is the only department in the corporate where somehow it's expected that you can do more using sheer magical talent. The CMO today is not just responsible for the Brand, the marketing machine, retention and a whole lot more, but as a manager, the CMO is responsible for building a department that can consistently achieve magical growth.

And we do try. In the fast-paced marketing environment where it is believed the sky's the limit, we are pushed to take bold steps and develop daring campaigns. We are constantly learning and improving, such is the nature of the modern marketing department. We are also regularly failing.

Here's what being a CMO feels like today:

3. Marketing technologies just keep getting more and more complicated.

4. My staff seems to mysteriously shrink in comparison to the tasks at hand.

5. The market keeps changing—darn it.

Failure? Of course! Failures are part of the process and we don't dwell on them. They are expected and get consumed so quickly that only the largest of them make a blip on our radar. And even those blips, we take in stride. We then continue on our course because we do not have time to look over our shoulders.

The best CMOs run their teams with a blend of mysticism and science that focuses on adaptation and the ability to pivot on a dime. We insist on the value of face-to-face as much as the value of data. Big data became all the rage just two years ago and people are still scrambling to understand and harness it, but frankly, not all of it has to be harnessed. If the marketing department is a sailboat in a race, we aim our bow and trim our sails. We look to our instruments—our radar—to make decisions, but we also must look one another in the eye when the wind and waves become unpredictable.

Not everything can be measured well, but a great marketing department is obsessed with trying to constantly calculate the cost of acquiring customers on each channel, and with understanding the potential lifetime value of each customer.

Marketing entails living with the unpredictable—in spite of all the data; it entails walking the line between surviving the process and mastering it—in spite of the fact that the elements of the modern day marketing process are constantly emerging, shifting, and disappearing.

Clearly, no marketer can ignore data. Those who have, died out as a species awhile back. But not having "all" the data is no excuse for not taking risks. Besides, you will never have "all" the data.

We have only just begun to marry big data to what we have always excelled at—persuading, winning over, seducing, dazzling, and converting. With our data and our dreamy CEO-inspired vision combined, we can set course and make our destination the next "it" place. We can get from Point A to Point Z quickly, but all along the way, ours will be the team that also uncovers new points of interest—sometimes by making mistakes.

Whether we have just graduated from an MBA program, or have been in the trenches for decades, we'll admit now that unless we are working for Proctor and Gamble—where everyone has been doing the same thing for years—nobody has experience in whatever it is we are doing, because whatever we are doing is new. Whatever we are doing Day One on the job or Day Three Thousand and One didn't exist five years ago. Nowadays, we are all inexperienced. This is something all marketers have to accept, at every level in the marketing department, if we want to manage resources properly and excel.

We cycle so quickly now. Three years ago, every CMO on the block was hiring social media gurus. Six months later, they were firing them. Today, we are bringing them back on. I've advised businesses that see a strategic value in SEO. SEO? Nowadays, it's not as relevant as a strategy, it's just something you get done. And of course, we have to talk about Facebook: It was only a few years ago that we were spending billions of dollars to get consumers to like our company pages. Then, literally overnight, Mark Zuckerberg said, "We're decreasing the amount of organic exposure that your company is going to get on Facebook to just about zero. From now on, you'll have to be paid to be seen."

Boom! Marketing moves like that. The wind is taken out of your sail and you are stuck on the crest of the wave. You can spend months

Today's innovative CMOs have a built-in R/D department that is always adjusting and developing new channels and new methodologies. Non-innovative CMOs who just run the department operationally, focusing on making the sale more efficiently (as they always have), get their butts kicked by the competition.

building an entirely new marketing methodology only to have it devastated by one announcement from one company. This is the new norm, and it doesn't matter if it's Facebook, or Twitter, or Google Plus (does anybody remember Google Plus?). Now, we grab some of whatever is *hot now*. We know it won't last long, so we ride that great wave while we can.

Do we lose unimaginable sums while atop some waves, and do we therefore fail? Yes, and yes. But today, this is the cost—and the rate—of marketers figuring things out. Some of our efforts pan out, others don't. What doesn't work, we might try a bit differently. What works, we stick to for as long as it is viable. This is the process.

This process of always adjusting doesn't encourage failure, but it does allow for it. Marketers, of all people understand the nature of people! People make mistakes. And although people are finicky, they also are creatures of habit, and are fundamentally uncomfortable with change. As a CMO, I know that stability on the job has never existed. Ten years ago, marketing cycles were longer, but none of us come to this profession if stability is a top priority.

Today, as opposed to ten years ago or even just two years ago, the instability in marketing is extreme—it is a real cause for anxiety. It is no longer possible to single out a system that works and tell your team, "Okay, we've figured out this one perfect channel and as long as we beat our competitors and excel at it, we're golden."

It might be the most dangerous and foolish confession I make, but here it goes: When I tell my team and my CEO I have things figured out for today, I know full well that tomorrow the rug might be pulled out from under me—and I'll have to start figuring things out all over again—from scratch.

After you learn that the entire narrative and strategy you have spent months building and delivering—successfully—will no longer be relevant as of end-of-this-business-day, nod your head and take a deep breath. Then, figure out what new resources you will need, determine where the bottleneck will be, and plan on delivering the big stuff within that impossible-CEO-determined timeframe, but accept that it does not have to be perfect. Make it great, and plan to refine it, but forget the word "perfect" as you have forgotten the word "stability."

This is agile marketing: You figure it out as you go and you accept the fact that by the time you perfect something, it will no longer be relevant.

Get your crew together and map out a course for moving forward. Know that all great marketers have paid the cost, and they always will. Know that when Volvo's marketing team had Jean-Claude Van Damme perform a split between two of its trucks gleaming sleek and gold in the sunlight, the time and money and brainpower they spent in production was part of the ongoing process. It doesn't matter that Volvo's marketing department has more money than yours, or if Van Damme performed his stunt in one perfect take or not: Volvo didn't get to that level of viral video production overnight. Marketers never stop re-examining, re-evaluating, doing,

A brand that knows how to be more agile in marketing than their competition has a major competitive advantage in today's rapidly changing marketplace.

and learning—whether they are working at Volvo level, or at Start-Up #9.

Many people claim to be seeking change, but in truth—again—most are change-resistant. In this aspect, maybe marketers really are mystical creatures. Those of us who make it in this field see change as an opportunity. Change offers us a chance to grab a share of the market, even from our biggest competitors. In the past, we'd think, "How can I compete with Google, Microsoft, or AT&T?" But now all of a sudden, the big guys can't maneuver the shifting seas as fast as we can.

Recruit an adaptable crew and manage change, and you will carry your ship along any wave—of any magnitude—as smoothly as those Volvo truck drivers, who rolled in reverse with a man standing between them.

Chapter Two

Marketing Is the Business

Why I'm Obsessed with the CPA, and Why You Should be Too

Though we stand here on planet Earth spinning a thousand miles per hour, we don't feel a thing. Pretty cool this force called gravity!

As a marketer, if you are worrying about the speed of change, you are worrying about the wrong thing. If you keep worrying about the ten thousand miles per hour we now cycle through daily on planet CMO, the universe is going to spit you out. Worry about getting the most you can out of what is working today and remain agile.

Everything changes. I repeat: Nothing stays the same. Even my job title—Chief Marketing Officer—didn't exist not too long ago. We used to refer to the VP of Marketing or the Director of Marketing, and of course, some companies still do, but here we are, in the

CMO Era. Heads of marketing departments are C-level now, because every company that wants to remain vital in the ever-crowded universe knows that marketing must cross all departments. Everything must pass through marketing. Without a CMO you risk obliteration via any number of black holes.

Just a few years ago, many businesses were still operating under the mindset: Here's a lead, take it and convert it. Today's CMO has to ask: "How do we create products that will sell themselves? How do we continually reinvent ways to excite people and create unique customer experiences? How do we create loyalty and promote evangelism?

Gone are the days where marketers developed leads and sales teams closed them—and gone too is the salesperson's ability to blame the marketer for supplying them with a "bad lead." Sales teams now recognize that marketing IS the business.

This doesn't mean we axe sales and advertising departments. This does mean all departments are becoming more entwined—no matter the size of a company or the number or days or decades it has existed. Fortunately, once everyone puts their departmental titles and egos aside, it is easier than ever to align, because there is less mystery and mythos surrounding our target consumers. Remember too, that even though marketing IS the business, marketers are not the "intuitive beasts" they once were. The playing field has been somewhat evened and integrated, via technology—via cold hard data.

Does sales need to know who is coming back to a website and who is truly a prospective customer versus a consumer merely looking for information? They need marketing. Does advertising need to see who is visiting the website and who is visiting the brick-and-mortar store and who is doing both? They need marketing. Does customer support need to know when to upsell a customer and when to nudge them to promote the brand? They need marketing.

True, marketing has not always controlled the numbers and the reports, but because numbers and reports are becoming increasingly more telling, they hold more value. Data is the Golden Ticket, or rather, the Golden Blueprint, in terms of how a company will design a chocolate factory that will attract frolicking consumers willing to spend, and repel consumers who do not go with the flow.

Of course, Amazon is the paragon company when it comes to revealing the power of marketing—there's not a salesperson to be found. And Fiverr works solely on a peer-to-peer system. But for all intents and purposes, most companies still require healthy input from a variety of teams—marketing, sales, and product. It's why most of us enjoy the game—we crave the humanity and the insanity of it!

What has changed for companies most urgently though, beyond human resources, is the relationship between the cost of manufacturing a product, the market value of that product, and the cost of marketing it. In the old days, the majority of the cost a company assumed in order to bring a product to market was in the manufacturing process itself. Back in the day, if you wanted to make a stronger cheaper plastic, it might take you fifty years, now it takes five. Why?

Now, there are far more opportunities to design and test a product on the market before it goes to mass production. We design and market much more rapidly than we manufacture, meaning, if you have an idea for a product, you design it. You test the waters. It's a hit? Great. Then get it made for a miniscule cost, with miniscule overhead, and with miniscule shipping costs. It's a dud? Toss it and go back to the drawing board.

What we're working with now is a combination of the cycles of innovation moving faster, in tandem with the prices of manufacturing dropping. The result is that the whole business model has flipped. Marketing is a science that provides a systemized solution to the following questions:

- How much can this client pay?

- What does the client need?

- How should I present the right product at the right time so that they pay the maximum potential value?

So, let's talk numbers instead of imagination, more science, less art. In the old days, you would take the cost of manufacturing, add your profit margin to it, and voila—there you'd have your retail price. In today's economy, you can work the other way round by imagining a product that a market segment wants, figuring out what value you could extract from it, and selling it to them at one price—while selling an almost identical product to another segment at another price.

What's the difference between the two models? In most cases the answer is marketing. Take toothpaste as an example: Almost all toothpastes are literally identical, so why the 600% price difference? Different market segments are willing to spend different amounts of money on toothpaste, so smart marketers created different packaging with different messaging to justify that price difference. One toothpaste calls itself the "new" formula, while the other is a "trusted" formula. The only *real* difference between the two products is the emotional value associated with the message.

You can also make the exact same product and package it in a slightly different way, thereby stacking your profit margins according to specific targets. In the digital world, it is that much easier, because the cost of creating different versions of your product is next to nothing and your ability to classify visitors and customers by personas is incredibly accurate. Salesforce is built this way: It is essentially the same service, but the more subscriptions a customer wants, the more the customer pays. Bringing in more value from one target costs Salesforce no more than it does for the other on the costs of goods—the difference in costs happens on the marketing end (CPA). So for Salesforce, as with all SaaS companies, the more expensive it is to get to the client, the more they charge.

Now this is not always the case. Marketers do have the power to determine and seek out only higher value consumers, and we should. As technology advances, we can weed out those consumers who aren't our highest performing consumers, and we can spend precisely what it takes to keep them, while upping the ante on the type of consumer we want to see more of—the type who will spend more on our products.

Our marketing plan starts with us asking: "Once we've located our potential target audience, how much will it take to market our product to them, and then how can we dress our product up to justify what it is we need to charge in order to make our profit margin?" In other words, the new model starts with the profit margin. We ask: Which audience can provide us the highest margin, and how much would it cost us to acquire such a customer? Only after we have the answers to those two questions do we then ask ourselves how much it will cost us to design, build, and deliver a matching product to this audience. From this point on, execution and scale are simply a function of keeping below our target CPA.

Getting to people who are willing to pay more for your product is where the greatest risk and greatest cost—but also the potential greatest reward—now lies. Marketers have the insight. What is the cost of acquiring these customers? How many customers can I get to by spending X?

Once you know the answers to these questions, you begin to build your model. You might be wrong sometimes—you might sometimes fail. But remember, all failures in the new marketing model rarely add up. As a CMO, you know failure is the cost of doing business. Move on. Cost of acquisition is at the center of all marketing models today, and not the cost of manufacturing—so invest in learning and in creating systems that help you determine where you need to scale up, and where you need to scale down.

Long ago, in a universe far away, marketers bemoaned this fact: "I know I'm throwing away at least half of my marketing budget, I just don't know what half."

We are all too good for that now. We have the power to engineer the profit margin we want. We can monitor now, in real time, how many leads are coming from Google advertising and how many are coming from another channel. From there, the question becomes: Now what profit margin do we want on this product, and how do we dress it up so that those we know are hungry for it and willing to spend more, will?

In scrutinizing the sources of our leads—we track landing pages, pricing pages, and all the pages in between—we can determine the price not just of what brought target customers there, but also the price of bringing them back. We can also predict what they might be willing to pay. From there, we can scale our manufacturing orders, again, in real time. Our main cost then, again, is acquisition—it is the purchase of potential customers.

This is the new way we talk about profit margins. Because we now put 99.999999% of our energies into the customer, we are talking about a philosophy that extends way beyond the old saw "The customer is always right." Improving profit margins relies heavily on personalization, and personalization involves traditional notions of customer satisfaction as well as pre-emptive notions of customer satisfaction. What do I mean by that? I mean, we marketers use our data, and consumers use theirs. Consumers are informed, they do know we are "onto them," and in turn, they know how to keep us on our toes. They know they're being courted every step of the way and won't hesitate to throw egg in our face—via the little blue bird of Twitter—if we make a misstep.

Marketers have the power now to perform profit margin jujitsu, but we should never break the data or the funnel down so much that we lose our flow. If you segment your funnel from Step A to Step P, you will foster disruption between the very people and teams you need working in unison. In strategizing for change, you don't want to build a ship where everyone working it has fractioned and acutely focused funnel vision. Leave the old dinosaur-like companies where they belong—in the dust, buried. We've established the fact—all marketers today must be agile.

We live in a time of constant change where we can make markets instead of merely taking advantage of them. Hold everyone on your team accountable for getting consumers to move from Point A to Point B, from Point B to Point C, and all the way through to the end. Hold everyone accountable to educating all leads toward a sale, and everyone profits.

Chapter Three

The Marketer's Guide to the Galaxy

Three Principles for marketing in the New Business Reality

Some say those of us promoting the idea that marketing is an entirely different beast today than it was yesterday are just sounding the alarm. We are overdoing it. Nothing is really new in marketing, they say, except the tools.

I disagree.

Yes, the fundamental tenets of human psychology in regards to human desire and the consumption of goods and services remain the same; but, there has been a critical shift in the way non-marketing C-level executives are beginning to grasp the necessity of understanding their company's marketing budget. Countless CEOs come up to me after I speak to this need and say: "I know every metric when it comes to my production line, but have never asked my VP of marketing how many opportunities she is responsible for, or how many she expects to bring in this quarter. I guess I never gave it much thought—before today."

And these are companies that are selling in the multi-million dollar range every month. They should want the added insight and power.

Many CEOs are beginning to tune in to the new marketing reality, but a few out there still think of marketing as a form of expansion: They think you put some money in the magazine ads, some money online, and some money in direct mail—and voila!

"Our marketing works," these CEOs will tell me, "but I don't know how.

And then they will say, "I want to know how now."

It is easier than ever to know how your marketing works and it is time for everyone to get on board and begin eating, sleeping, and waking marketing. Alright, maybe that's just me overdoing it—but the point is, there is no excuse for anyone to continue doing their job without understanding the impact of the Three Principles of the New Marketing Reality on their company's success.

The Three Principles are: Markets are Transparent, Everything is Measurable, and the Cost Per Acquisition (CPA) is Similar for All Competitors.

Principle One: Markets are Transparent

When I outline this principle in a seminar, I always hear from a few CMOs: "But I don't want transparency. I don't want people to know what I'm doing, or what's working for my company and what's not. We've got our secret sauce, and we want to keep it that way!"

Any time I hear those words: "We want to keep it that way," I cringe.

I say, "No, it's definitely the other way around. You've brought in X-number of leads, and by linking those leads directly to a Y-dollar amount of revenue, you can ask for a bigger budget. You can measurably demonstrate to your CEO and investors that you are not replaceable. You become someone who must have a say in your organization's decision-making process. Transparency is empowering!"

I also know that beneath some of the protest and discomfort with transparency, is the fear people have with their performance being measured.

Clearly, we have more information and better access to it. We have the ability to try out a variety of approaches on a very large scale using a simple but powerful AB test. And we are discovering that different models can work in places we didn't think they might work before. For instance, we are learning we can use B2C marketing techniques in the B2B world, when before it was assumed that emotion didn't count as much in B2B marketing as value propositions did. We are learning, today, thanks to transparency and our ability to measure, that some of the assumptions we have been making for decades have been wrong.

To me this is thrilling!

Markets are transparent, and marketers are too. Why fear everyone knowing what you are up to, when you can see what they are up to just as easily?

There are so many services online now that will tell you anything you want to know about any company. Instantly, you know what Company X is doing, what technologies they are using, what organic keywords they are running on, what keywords they are advertising on, and how much they are bidding on those keywords. You can figure out what marketing automation system they use and get copies of all their customer communications—and this is only the legal stuff. For our competitors overseas who don't need or want to comply with our legal code, it's not too hard to get a copy of the competitor's entire customer database.

It used to take years of research, or an expensive consultancy firm, to figure out what the bigger players were up to. That is no longer the case—we have equal access to "the cutting edge" thanks to transparency and technology. In a game where it is obvious what everyone is doing, what everyone is charging, and what everyone's unique selling proposition is, all we have to do is figure out the next audience to target.

We then strategize according to Principle Two.

Principle Two: Cost Per Acquisition (CPA) is Roughly the Same for All Competitors

Principle One says, "If everything is transparent, we're all essentially on the same playing field. The cost for me to acquire traffic is roughly the same as it is for my competition, as is the cost of acquiring customers. This means it's a matter of who is slightly better at doing what they do."

There is an obvious realization that comes next: There is no way to build a business on being better at acquiring traffic. The only way to succeed is to have better pricing power.

When you go online to assess who is acquiring traffic, you will always find somebody who is willing to outbid you. How are they doing it? They might be losing money because they cannot measure well. Or, they might still be working the old mindset of: "We pay X-amount because X is just the cost of doing business, right?"

Or, and this third possibility is the worst one for you and the one you want to start paying close attention to: Your competitor might know how to monetize traffic better than you; they might be doing something different that is allowing them to extract more value from your shared target audience. When this seems to be the case, work the transparency and technology angle to gather all the insight you can.

Of course, yet another challenge exists today that didn't exist just a short time ago: Because it is so easy for marketers today to target consumers by persona rather than by interest alone, we are all competing not just against our direct competition, but against anyone who is willing to pay to get in front of the same audience as ours.

Principle Three: Anything Can Be Measured

Marketers still talk about billboards—we will always talk about billboards even if we know most people have their heads down now, buried eye-deep in their phones and tablets. The issue with billboards is this: Marketers will tell you, "We can't measure the effectiveness of a billboard ad, but we're going to put them up all across the city because we know they work. The same is true of the booth we put up at trade shows. How can we measure our booth's effectiveness? We can't."

I disagree. I believe anything can be measured. You just need to figure out how to measure it as best you can.

Anything can be measured and we need to measure, so with the more challenging measurements, such as billboards and trade show booths, the first question we have to ask is: How do we collect signals that will give us a good working estimate of who is paying attention to our message? And what will these signals be?

We then challenge that estimate, and try to prove it one way or another. For instance, there are no sensors on billboards. There is no way to count how many people rest their eyes on your billboard every minute, or for how many seconds they remain enraptured. You don't know specifically, but you do know roughly how many people pass your billboard daily: 20,000 people pass it daily and 200 people might be interested in your product. You should be getting an extra 10 leads a day, out of which, if you ask them, one should mention, "I saw your great billboard."

Of course, you have to be careful how you collect feedback, because there is always a tendency to see what you want to see in order to prove your own case, i.e. "Our billboard rocks! I knew it! We need to put up five more and we'll have 50 leads a day."

Caution! Hold up! No! Not quite. The point I'm making is you have to go into every "less measurable" approach with a bit more gusto and a heightened awareness of whatever statistical signals are coming your way. Before you go to that conference and spend $50,000 to put up a booth, establish your KPIs, know how many leads you intend to collect and what your cost per lead will be. It costs everybody the same $50K to put up a conference booth, so how are you going to do a better job than the booths you are sandwiched between, in terms of meeting your KPIs? Start by figuring out what your CPA is, and how many leads you need to bring in to justify the $50K expenditure.

What I'm trying to say here is that marketers need to be disruptive. Your booth costs the same as your competitor's across the aisle from you. So what are you going to do with your booth that is different and that will allow you to gather twice the leads that they do?

By laying out your expected results beforehand, you can gauge how close you came, and can then take it to the next level. The effectiveness of a booth can be measured if you are really focused on performance. Focus is key here: Do not focus on the cost of setting up a booth at your top-notch conference, focus on the cost per lead and make it work to your advantage so that next time a conference rolls around, you and your team can present some cold hard numbers to your CEO and blow his or her mind—"You measured the effectiveness of a booth! But how?"

The Three Principles of the New Marketing Reality do not require that we reinvent the wheel, but we had better understand that the wheel is spinning faster. Because of this new spin and the force it is generating, we must shift our focus. Even when we are looking at the "easier to measure" parameters, such as Google Ads, we need to scrutinize the right thing: We need to scrutinize the cost per lead and the cost per sale, not just the cost per click, which for some reason so many marketers still do.

Given the pace we have to maintain today, there is no time to waste. Half the battle in doing things just slightly better than our competitors and gaining the competitive edge is won in knowing what signals and measurements hold the most value, and how to leverage them most—swiftly and with confidence.

Chapter Four

Managing Creativity I

Disruptive Content and Your Competitive Edge

When my CEO asked me to pivot very rapidly our company's focus from small business to enterprise sales, I had to decide almost overnight on a strategy for building growth.

I knew I could base the new model on acquisition, meaning I could buy traffic in the form of highly targeted customers of high value. We could pay a lot of money for these customers, convert them quickly, and come out looking good; however, things would no doubt become too expensive to maintain and our profit margin, instead of growing over time, would actually shrink. If I were concerned only with checking "Huge Rapid Success" off my list of accomplishments, I could have done this—I could have bought the traffic. But quick fixes, as in most aspects of life, don't work when you care about long-term growth. The better way to succeed in the long run is to generate a long-rolling wave of traffic and ride it out.

Here is the basic challenge we marketers face: Most products are boring—they are just another product. This is particularly true in the B2B world, even more so than in enterprise sales, where no one understands what you are talking about in the first place. The ideal scenario is to create products that are fascinating in their own right, so that people are naturally drawn to them. This is one of the CMO's roles, but this vision is only realistic to a certain point.

Most often, the way we create online movement toward our product is not by using the product itself, but by using the branded content we create. The product itself is just a product—it is the content marketing that counts now, literally, as a magnet for your audience.

When we adhere to the strategy of content marketing, it means we sometimes must work within a Catch-22: If our product is a B2B corporate product—that is, it isn't a snazzy or sexy new music device or a fun cutting-edge app—we have to speak the language of our "boring product" corporate audience. In these kinds of situations, we must create our own disruption. We did exactly this when we created a brand built around our own magazine, *The Daily Lead.*

With *The Daily Lead*, we started building content that would attract all the various personas we were interested in—and it is working very well, because it is scalable. Over time, as long as our content stays strong, the cost of acquisition will shrink. Bringing people in via content, we not only start the wave rolling in terms of initial product intrigue, but we get our audience to give us their contact information (not always an easy task) and then are able to develop further interest in our product.

Thinking disruptively about content has given us a competitive edge.

Being disruptive does not require reinventing the wheel—it simply requires looking around. Most of the content you see out there for certain corporate products is insanely boring only because there is a conception that if you want to appear professional when talking to enterprises, your content has to "look the part," that is, it has to be dull. But this conception is a misconception, and this is why *The Daily Lead* is successful: We saw nine out of ten of our competitors talking to our audience the same way—so we took off in the opposite direction, and so far, today, it is working.

Marketers these days need to be as disruptive as startups are. We need to think like startups do: How do we create experiences that are so unique, that they will not only attract attention, but that our competitors won't be able to imitate these experiences easily—or quickly enough?

Precisely because of our size—we are not one of the biggest players on the planet—we can free ourselves from doing things according to the status quo. Most companies can do this too—break free—or they could, if only they made the choice to risk getting a little egg on their face once in a while. It turns out, we did not fail with *The Daily Lead*, but we could have.

We decided to be disruptive when we said, "All the content out there is boring. Let's make our content not boring. How? What's the opposite of boring? Emotionally engaging. Okay. How do we make content that is emotionally engaging? We add colorful artwork and make a few big claims. We may not be perfect at it, but we'll improve along the way. Alright then! Let's make our content wild, bombastic, and aggressive. Let's find the people who can create this kind of content."

But there is more to this thinking. As CMO, I need to think about how to create a *system* that is inherently more creative than that of our competitor's, otherwise they will simply poach our top talent and beat us at our own game. We can't just sit back and kick our feet up as soon as we've got the clever and creative people and ideas, we also need to figure out how to run our show cheaper and more creatively than the competition.

Disruptiveness also applies to operational thinking: If your competition is spending $5,000 over three months to crank out one eBook, how can you build an operational "machine" that cranks out (creative, quality) eBooks in under a month and costs you only $1,000?

People who can get into a wave like ours and ride it will not come cheap—we know this. We knew we had to find people more talented than our competitors' people, and we had to claim them and keep them. We almost had to market to the content marketers—but we managed. And then in fact, once we had our talent, we figured out a way to operationally make better, higher-quality content, cheaper than everybody else. When we managed that, our competitive edge kicked in further and we began to outpace our competition.

Staying lean is crucial as a CMO. Marketers have to be very fit to get through the day. We go to the gym before work, but then our work is also a type of gym. We have to be mentally charged and flexible.

The Daily Lead worked because we made a few predictions in the early stages of the game when setting up our strategy and execution—which frankly, are not very different in my mind. Yes, it was challenging to predict how successful we would be, because it would all be based on talent—and talent is often subjective. How would we know how emotionally engaging our content would be? How would we know how our audience would react to something so different?

We don't understand all elements of most equations, but because markets are transparent and we have our own history and proven ability to achieve a certain kind of KPIs, we can make some basic assumptions. We decided we wanted 20% quarterly growth, so we asked, "What is the average lead generation rate out there in the market?" We found it was between 1% and 3%, so we targeted the high end. We rooted out all the numbers and facts we needed, put it all up on a spreadsheet, then trusted those numbers, plus our guts, and we executed. All the while, we kept a close eye on the variables in the formula that represented our assumptions.

For many startups, especially in high-growth companies, many times the biggest challenge for CMOs is unrealistic expectations from the CEO, the board, and the shareholders. Somebody will come up with a number out of nowhere and will tell the CMO they have to grow by some number, say 30% per month. Why? Because a spreadsheet says so. Part of the reason I was able to turn the ship so quickly was because of experience and confidence. But all CMOs, whether at start-ups or at long-established firms, can do the same if they ask the question: Are we going to be able to execute this strategy with our resources and with our managerial abilities? And do we have the ability to attract talent?

Attracting and hiring talent can be a huge challenge. But more importantly, once you have your talent in place, how do you manage it? When we set out on course with *The Daily Lead*, we were seeking to create emotionally engaging business content. The question I had to answer was: What kind of environment will pull this kind of creative output out of everyone on the team, whether they are the most talented at this task, or not?

Clearly, when you are trying to encourage creativity, you don't want to provide exact guidance. To encourage my team to get in touch with their emotions and their gut-feelings, I asked them open-ended questions. When they showed me work and asked, "What do you think?" I responded by asking, "How would you feel if you read this or saw this?" and then, "If you feel that way, do you think your audience—who may not be similar at all to you, by the way—will feel the same?"

"I don't know what the result might be," someone would say. And to that, I'd say, "I hired you. You're smart. Take a risk."

When managing creative talent, I always let them know our work—marketing—is not about the hard numbers or the hard results. I promote the process of getting to the result, and my teams always know that it's okay to fail along the way. This doesn't mean I allow repeated mistakes—I don't. But as long as I see someone is working hard, taking risks, and learning from the mistakes they make, we keep moving forward.

I encourage my talent to be very shrewd, very quick, and very suspecting. Once they have fortified themselves this way, we don't have to worry about figuring things out all the way ahead of time. The marketing cycles move far too quickly anyway, for us to waste time "making sure we've got it 100% figured out." I feel sorry for companies still working under this model. No! Just get clear on what you want, and get comfortable with the notion you will tackle disturbances as they come.

Building a team that works together is no walk in the park, but if you draw in people who are curious, instill in them confidence to take risks, and do not compromise on your ultimate vision—i.e. creating more emotionally engaging content for a typically non-emotionally engaged audience—you will have everything you need to outpace your competition.

Chapter Five

Managing Creativity II

The Two Teams and The Four Cs

Some CMOs are probably expert at hiring top talent right off the bat and building All-Star teams, no sweat. Me, I must confess, I have made a few hiring mistakes in the past. And because I dread letting people go, I had to learn the hard way. Interviews will always be tricky, because along with market transparency comes "What to Expect in an Interview" transparency, and candidates come in well-prepared and in some cases, well-rehearsed. You hire them and put them to the test, and some exceed your expectations and some stop trying right after the first paycheck.

What I do know now though, in terms of how to manage top talent once I've curated it is first of all, there are two types of teams you can build: the Specialist Team and the Multitasking Team. In the Specialist Team, each member is highly knowledgeable and talented in one field or skill. The advantage of this team structure is that you've got individuals who are very good at one thing, and are focusing entirely on excelling at it. The drawback is that they are not as good at doing all the other things that we know are required to stay competitive, and will likely not grow their repertoire. Of course, that's why you have everyone else: Juan is great at design aesthetics, Mary is great at coding, Raoul is a fabulous writer, and Paloma excels at social media. When building the Specialist Team, you just stack them up and manage how they work together.

The Multitasking Team, on the other hand, consists of individuals with certain inclinations or proclivities, but nobody is really "a pro" at one specific thing. Everyone on this team is versatile. Your designer might not know how to Tweet, but has razor-sharp intuition as to why and when people will engage with Twitter. Your coder might also be driven to get contact information from X-number of people by the end of the day, and will put in her two cents on how the team can do that. If you are looking to build a disruptive marketing department, then creating multi-tasking teams is the way to go.

My mistake, in the past, was that I didn't understand I couldn't ask a specialist to multitask, and vice versa. The specialist's objectives are to do what they do even more deeply. Expanding their horizons is not relevant to them, whereas, multitaskers thrive on being jacks-of-all-trades. Sometimes then, it is a mistake to assume that if somebody isn't performing to your expectations, or if an entire team seems off-kilter, it is because you didn't hire well and nobody is capable. It means perhaps you didn't build the type of team in which everyone would flourish; you didn't create the environment that would bring out the best in the people you did in fact, very carefully vet. Once you understand the difference between specialists and multitaskers, it is not only easier to hire more wisely, but it is also easier to let people go—and you need to be able to do both in order to maintain your competitive edge.

Once you have built your team, whichever type is best-suited to the particular project, task-at-hand, or company culture, you can then start getting them used to the fact you will always ask the question, "What is everyone else doing?" followed by, "Let's do the opposite."

No Copycatting

My teams now know how to think, create, and move—in unison—because they know the first of my Four Cs rules is: No Copycatting. "Wait," they always say, "if Strategy X is working for everyone else, why wouldn't we implement Strategy X too?"

If you have someone onboard who is not quite catching onto the logic behind the No Copycatting rule, show them the "Opposite George" episode of Seinfeld. We are coming into an era where we can't assume everyone has seen that show, but whether they are twenty-four or forty-four, everyone can relate to the notion of how they might be "more successful" today if they had taken a 180-degree turn yesterday.

At every juncture then, see where the crowd is heading or is stuck, and turn away. If we were to take our company literature and change the heading to the name of our competitor's company, would it still make sense? Nine times out of ten, the answer is yes because we are similar. This is our reality. I instill in my marketing team the notion that in this sea of voices that all sound the same, the stakes rest on being different—even if it means being just slightly different.

It's our job to make our company stand out and if we are all paying roughly the same dollar for that conference booth, advertising space, and CPA—and if we have roughly the same size marketing department and profit margin, one way we can distinguish ourselves from the crowd revolves around features: "Okay, they have a feature which is good for A, so we will create a feature that is good for B."

But the more interesting approach, after sussing out who has the better features, ultimately comes down to a question of: "How do we, as a marketing department, implement a tactic or a strategy that allows us to outpace our competition? If it is easy enough to track our competitor's spending and targets and so on, how do I, as CMO, work behind the scenes to better manage my talent?"

If you can figure out how to better manage your talent, you can gain the competitive edge. Because we are in competition nowadays not just with our direct competitors—the ones who all sound the same—but for space and attention in general—whatever mechanism we can use to gain that edge is critical. Managing talent is hard—so get great at it, and nobody will be able to catch up with you. If they do, in the meantime, you will have moved even further ahead.

We are in competition with those in our field and those outside of it, but most importantly, we are in competition with ourselves. I never stop asking, "How do we do better? How do we make a difference?" because a new reality is being created every day, and with it, a new benchmark. What was innovative yesterday has become standard today, and we have to innovate again. I strive to create the kind of marketing department that is constantly moving and accelerating, without fear of spinning off into oblivion.

In this crazy whirlwind of staying ahead of the competition and following the No Copycat rule, I rely on the second and third rule of The Four Cs to keep my team inspired and grounded: I encourage my talent to stay Curious, and I provide them extra Confidence.

Curiosity

Curiosity can be inherent in our nature, but you can also create a team atmosphere and company culture that invites questions and pushes everyone to seek answers together. Make sure each person at your table feels free to discuss their wildest ideas, and their mistakes, openly. Let's challenge assumptions and always be engaging with people outside our direct spheres of interest. If people and personas are who we are "after," that is, who we must engage, it is to our advantage—professionally and personally—to understand what drives, attracts, and repels everyone we have set sights on.

Confidence

It takes the Third C, Confidence to authentically and continually pose questions—to essentially say, "I'm not sure. I don't know. Can you teach me? Can you help me? I have no idea what will happen next."

Confidence in taking risks is critical to promoting and managing creativity.

Now, when you are dealing with an accounting department, you can't say, "Hey, why don't we do our accounting differently this year and submit a different kind of report to the FCC." This kind of risk is obviously not good and possibly not legal! We don't like that. What we do like is instilling in our marketing department the confidence to take risks in terms of asking: "What would happen if…?"

I see the "anti-if" management style all the time: In a risk-averse marketing department, results are the only thing that counts. In this type of environment, not only is curiosity stifled—because the eye is trained directly on one prize only—but the fear of failure is heightened as well. If you are judged solely on end-of-day results, you will never take risks. Run from this type of culture. It is a dying culture and one you certainly do not want to be in charge of.

Give yourself and your marketing department ample room to "try stuff" in a proportionate and appropriate manner, and to learn from mistakes. People flourish when they are confident that the first attempt at something new, even if it adds up to zilch, won't land them at the unemployment office. No! Instill that old adage, "If at first you don't succeed, try, try again," and keep your managerial eye on how well each team member is learning from mistakes.

Small mistakes leave me completely unfazed, because I know without them, we are very likely to fall into copycat syndrome. No Copycatting requires, ironically, the curiosity of a cat, complemented by the confidence of a cat. Cats honestly do not give a damn when they miss a jump, do they?

My response after someone on my team has made a genuine

effort based on a "What if...?" approach, but has "failed," is "Oh, that's interesting."

We'll even celebrate the mistakes we learn the most from.

Of course, what isn't tolerated is sweeping mistakes under the rug or being defensive. My management style aims to maintain Curiosity, build Confidence, avoid Copycatting, and encourage accountability. So, fourth of the Four Cs:

[No] Compromise

There is No Compromise on not learning from mistakes. Make the same mistake repeatedly, and we will have the "Seems like a bad fit" conversation nobody wants to have.

Marketing is less about the mystical, and more about hard work. It demands making decisions and taking action according to a learning curve—one that is quite often steep, but never impossible to ascend. We create our KPIs, achieve them, then raise the bar. Each time we raise the bar, we force ourselves to learn and improve. There is No Compromise either, on hard work and constant revision.

That said, while we do reboot our vision every time we learn from a mistake or up the ante in terms of KPIs, there is No Compromise on our ultimate vision, and as CMO, I am the one who decides what that ultimate vision is. I put to the test: Is the choice I am about to make serving my Vision, or is it leading me away from it?

Once you know what you want to build your competitive edge on, everybody needs to sign on. Of course, outside your team, you might have to rely on people that don't quite get it. For example, I outsourced once (and only once) a design agency that insisted they knew design better than I did. That was true—but what is also true is that nobody knows better than I do what my vision for a particular project, team, or company is. If I've decided our competitive edge entails creating more emotionally engaging content and a designer insists on work that feels rigid or otherwise out-of-sync with my vision, I will not budge. Only when the designer gets it right and presents me with my emotionally engaging material, will I be satisfied.

So, here we are as CMOs, flexible when it comes to ABCD and F, and yet stating there will be No Compromise on X. Leadership has to be giving on one hand, and very, very firm on the other. Be clear with your team about your vision, but allow them infinite ways and attempts at getting there.

This does not mean you hold brainstorming sessions that last hours, days, and weeks. Brainstorming, in fact, is in my mind, often a waste of time. Why? Frankly, because more often than not, brainstorming sessions reinforce patterns. Even when the best intentions are laid out and in the beginning, people come up with different and thrilling possibilities, very quickly someone dominant starts bringing everyone into line. Brainstorming sessions have become overused and misused, and frequently result in alignment.

Instead, again, I like to encourage No Copycatting. At the end of the day, maybe everyone still uses banner ads and social media. Everybody uses the same kind of call to action, because it has been tried and proven. But, if everybody uses the same approach, how do we know what other approaches are out there, and whether or not they might work better? If someone comes to me with an idea that sounds a little crazy, my ears perk up: Why do you think it might work? How are you going to make sure it does? How much money and time do you need to try and prove it?

Alternately, I'll say, "Try to prove that it doesn't work and come back to me next week."

With banner ads, for instance, we proved most media experts wrong when it came to selling business software. The general consensus amongst all the gurus was a flat one-size-fits-all mentality: You have to have moving graphics in your banners. A lot of these experts came from the gaming and gambling industries, or from the kind of industries that rely heavily on media buying and performance marketing. Yes, when you are promoting a casino, animated ads work very well; but, when you are trying to sell business software or a business solution, moving ads seem less reputable. We proved static ads worked.

That said, I never assume that what has worked three times for my team will work a fourth time, or that what made one project a huge success won't fall flat with another. If somebody tells me adamantly: "Email marketing is all spam. You will destroy your reputation if you buy email lists," I listen—it could be true, but not always.

As a manager, I constantly want to fuel the creative process. As soon as I see a pattern start to emerge, I go on high alert. Even if this pattern is solid and to continue doing the same thing would probably work out fine, I don't want "fine." There is no risk in "fine." Besides, I have waited too long before and when crisis hit—that is, our pattern became suddenly irrelevant overnight—everyone had to scramble. I don't set out to revise patterns for the fun of it—or for the sake of creativity and innovation alone—but whenever I see one emerging, I point it out and ask my team to reflect on what theory and what actions landed us here. Why have we been doing XYZ, and is Reason ABC really the right reason that it's been working?

Recently, for example, we took a chunk of data regarding our Tweets. The data seemed to reveal that people were responding to our Tweets at night, therefore, the natural next step would be to fortify our night Tweets. "But," I said, "before we make a decision, let's try to disprove the correlation."

What we discovered was that at midnight, Twitter sends out its 'Here's what you missed during the day' message, and some people were coming our way only for that reason—not due to any particular genius on our part, or content we had created.

The point is, eye-opening moments can happen when you ask your team to re-examine patterns. Some will prove true and will require investment; some won't. I had no clue what was happening with the night Tweet pattern that had emerged before I questioned it, I simply questioned it. I asked my team to re-examine their way of thinking and their readiness to take next steps before they could cement any "evidence" into a firm opinion.

When somebody says: "I've done this for twenty years and I can tell you that this is always the case," turn as fast as you can in the opposite direction.

There is no more "always," especially in marketing and managing your competitive edge.

Chapter Six

The All-Seeing CMO:

Using the Steps, Shape, and Velocity of Your Funnel to Forecast

Many CMOs approach marketing by asking: How do we build a strategy? How do we focus our department? How do we meet our KPIs? They set up their funnel and some kind of measurement, their team accomplishes more, then they accomplish more—*better*, and the organization grows.

"Sounds good to me," you're thinking, but here's what I think: If this standard approach to marketing is not carefully managed, your department is at risk of becoming less responsibility-focused and too task-focused. All will appear shiny on the outside for a while, but if you take a careful look beneath the surface, you'll see that everyone in your department has wound up dedicated to conducting a series of tasks—they are churning out the weekly newsletter and are talking about how it's supposed to generate this amount of traffic—and maybe it's succeeding at that measure—but look closely: Your team has lost their mojo, their flow.

Your funnel is the heart and soul of your department, and if you want to predict how well and how long a marketing campaign is going to live, you have to consider the three key aspects of your funnel: Steps, Shape, and Velocity.

In a task-focused marketing department, gravity will pull even the best talent down. Consider it your duty from this day forward to defy gravity. When we place the funnel at the very center of our marketing department, it means we don't have to fret and fuss over how many people clicked on our promotional email or what the click-through ratio is: What we truly have to care about—what we truly do care about—is how many people moved from one step of the funnel to the next. Marketing is all about this energy, this force, this mojo.

The funnel is people—it is people at different steps. The funnel is manifested by certain actions people take, or by events they engage in, or by visits they make to certain assets. When we see, for example, that somebody has read our eBook, we call that "interest." When somebody requests a demo, we call that something else. Our funnel needs to be less focused on action than it is on the performance of assets. Meaning, if I have an asset such as a newsletter, I ask: How is it performing? How are people interacting with it? I question not so much the asset itself, but what's happening in the gaps in-between "instances of assets."

I ask: How is my department moving people from one asset to the next—in a proper sequence—rather than simply checking off on some task-oriented list: "Five articles read by five thousand people."

My talent might produce fifty Pulitzer-worthy articles per month, but if these articles do nothing but keep a portion of five thousand people in the same level of the funnel, it isn't good for business—or rather, it is not good enough for business.

To cure my department of any task-focused mindset they might have picked up along the way, I refocus their attention past creating a clickable newsletter, to leading as many people as they can from one step in the funnel to the next.

The funnel is shaped as it is for a reason—funnel shape is one aspect of marketing that will never change, no matter how much things do change: You start by attracting a lot of people at the top of the funnel, and you lose some along the way. As you descend into the funnel, you pull in fewer and fewer people, at some point the rate of loss is drastically reduced, and from there you follow a steeper line.

For instance, if half the people coming to your website are looking for something they need, most of us would agree that it would be terrible if half of those people spoke to your "salesperson" and then left—because normally, you want the rate of loss at the top of the funnel to be as small as possible. However, in some cases, with some products and services such as high-end luxury goods, you want the rate of loss to be as high as possible at the top of the funnel, so that you can then focus the majority of your efforts on the few who remain.

Either way, in building your funnel, you've got to have clarity as to what happens down the road. If everyone on your team is given the sole duty to push as many people as he or she can from their singular step (aka their KPI) to the next—you may experience a blockage down the line. The person at the pricing page has to be in touch with the sales team, and vice versa, not only for feedback, but in order to help determine the best shape for the funnel. It might not be to your advantage to allow all visitors to see your pricing page, or you may need separate pricing pages—one for corporate and another for non-corporate people. You might have a case where Caroline sets customer expectation on the pricing page that your product is worth $100 a month, but Renata in sales wants to sell the product for ten times that amount. Even if $1000 is completely comprehensible, if you have exposed your customers to $100 at an early stage in the funnel, you are now in a bind. Your funnel cracks.

When I was asked to develop our new brand, I did so via our blog (and newsletter), *The Daily Lead.* I wanted to specifically target senior marketing managers via content marketing. Once visitors began showing up, I had to determine who they were—I knew nothing about *The Daily Lead* visitors at first, so I didn't know if they were the audience I wanted, and therefore, I didn't know quite how to move them. In order to gain more access to my visitors, I needed time to collect more data, so I offered an eBook. Our team commissioned a set of eBooks and tested them. The people who bit, we were able to determine, were marketing managers interested in the customer life cycle and in managing funnels.

Success!

But the truth is—and here is my confession—I was not interested in the asset itself. The eBook itself was irrelevant to me, it was just a magnet. I skimmed it over, saw it looked good, and moved on to what our next magnet at the next step, might be. The eBook served its purpose: It allowed me to move visitors down the funnel based on the personal information they shared: company name, job title, and email address. At this point then, my target audience and I were actively engaged.

If I had read the eBook from first to last page, I might have wasted precious time creating a "best-selling" asset, rather than focusing on how to move my now-engaged targeted audience down the funnel. I've seen too many Content Marketing Managers spend too many resources making sure their content is top-notch, but the bottom line is, they shouldn't care too much about what's inside the eBook or any asset, as long as it is bringing their target audience further into the funnel in a way they can be ID'ed (and of course as long as all brand and legal guidelines are being met).

The fundamental first few stages of the funnel haven't changed, and won't: Attention, interest, desire, action. You cannot create action without desire. You can't create desire without interest. And you can't spark interest without grabbing someone's attention. Ultimately, you have to figure out what assets or what behaviors elicit movement each step of the way.

The shape of the funnel is important. Essentially the question is: How much does it cost me to handle each step? If the major costs are in acquiring traffic at the top of the funnel, for instance, and not at steps below where everything becomes computerized, I might have minimal costs in the lower funnel. In that case, I'm incentivized to push as much traffic as I can down the funnel right away. Alternately, in models like the B2B model where the major costs are incurred mid-funnel, we want to escalate our efforts there. In this case, I also want to minimize the number of prospects who get mid-funnel, because from then on, they will cost me money.

Obviously, not everybody coming into a funnel is going to come out of it as a positive conversion. There is a limit to how many people we can sell to. You have to decide if you want to start losing people on purpose early on, or want to lose them down the road. Look at the CPA for each step and once the CPA gets to be expensive, target minimizing losses from there.

It's up to you to determine whether your funnel will be narrow or steep. What angles do you want it to have? You can imagine a funnel that starts very wide at the top, narrows down very rapidly, and then becomes very steep. Alternately, you can build a funnel that is more consistent from step-to-step, its angles decreasing more slowly. Your funnel can resemble more of a cone, or more of a tube, depending on the steps you build into it and the rate in which you want to move people from the top to the bottom.

Let's look at that rate: How fast are people moving from one step to the next, and how fast would you like them to move? What is your funnel velocity?

> Let's back up a moment first.
> Why does your website exist?
> It's a crucial part of my funnel.
> Is it? Okay, how?

Older industrial companies might not fully understand the need for a website, but most have one anyway. "Oh sure, people just want to see what the company's about," they'll say, considering their website the equivalent of a brochure.

Every single asset you own has one primary purpose: To move your audience down the funnel to the next step. Every single asset must therefore be optimized toward that goal.

This is a classic case of flawed thinking. The proper thinking is: At what stage of the funnel is somebody going to come to the website? What are they seeking and how do I give it to them? This line of questioning leads to the sole purpose of any website, and though finding the right answers might be complex, you need to find them.

Does your website need a blog, and if so, why? Having a website and a blog and even stellar content add up to little if you don't know how to augment, leverage, and manage these elements. I've seen a lot of companies run into trouble when the person responsible for maintaining the company blog is measured solely by how much content they produce. How much content you produce is irrelevant when you're managing the funnel as the heart and soul of a company and are instilling in your team that what counts most is how many people move on to the next step in the funnel, and how rapidly they do so.

The point is, there is a huge difference between being asset focused and being action focused. Actions are manifested as events—they are essentially digital signals that hit our marketing automation or CRM system and declare, "Person X did Y."

When we look at this in our database—and we do look all the time—we can begin define people on a very detailed level. We can see what steps they take, and where we lose them. If most people engage with three blog posts before we move them on to the next step, we have that figured out. There could be multiple funnels and multiple steps, but the clearer we become about how many steps it takes for somebody to move from one step to the next, the better we become at getting them there—meaning our funnel velocity increases and improves.

The faster we move people through the funnel, the less loss we have and the less resources we have to spend. A slicker funnel means that we're getting leads to sales. Furthermore, once you know the velocity of your funnel, you can make critical planning and management predictions.

When you use your funnel to forecast that barring WWIII, you'll be doing really well two quarters from now, you can better reallocate your department's budget. You can even decrease your budget from time-to-time, which goes against all popular wisdom. Maybe you see

Measuring funnel velocity as a core KPI is a sign that you have good control of the customer experience. Focusing on improving your funnel velocity directly impacts marketing and sales ROI.

a fixed capacity for production, meaning you have three maxed-out factories; or, your sales team currently has all the leads they can handle. Never spend extra money just to bring more people down the funnel that you can't service.

There could also be a capacity issue in terms of technology—maybe it's going to take three months to scale up new servers; or, perhaps your customer support team is being overhauled and this is not the time to grow your product. This might be a good time to invest, or to say, "We're going to meet the quota three months from now, so we're deciding not to grow more. How about we improve the quality of the department rather than the quantity? Let's try to improve the average sale price. Instead of bringing more leads, let's try to upsell the leads that do come in."

These are the discussions you want to have rather than just do more, do more, do more.

The problem is, many marketing departments fall back do more, do more, do more, because they don't have a clear view of the steps, shape, and velocity of the funnel they are working in, or they don't recognize the need to change things up from time to time. For some audiences, all you need is a basic funnel with five steps; other times, you need one with ten-steps. Whether you're building a simple or complex funnel, it's critical to know what steps people are at in your customer life cycle and what steps people want to take. You can no longer get away with saying, "Well, I know my customers are in my funnel and I know things are happening, I just don't know why, when, or how."

You can begin to get a grasp on the why, when, and how, even with a very simple three-step funnel:

1. Arrive at website, visit pricing, leave website.

2. Arrive at website, read about the product, leave.

3. Compare pricing with competitors, come back, purchase.

Three steps—and the first thing you look at is how many people you are losing between step one to two, then between step two to three, and finally between step three to purchase.

> Every contact in your marketing automation needs to be tagged by the funnel step they are in currently in. This tagging process is no longer just about leads—everyone must be tracked, tagged, and followed and a corresponding action must be taken to move them down to the next step, or to kick them out.

Analyze what's happening in your basic funnel, then start building departments and refocusing your existing departments. Figure out the step one to step two losses, and test until you land on what closes that gap—then add your test result as a fourth step, in between steps one and two. Close all the gaps in this way, and test your more complex funnel.

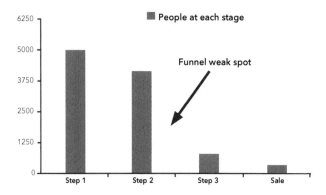

Don't be afraid to break your funnel up in to as many as ten or twelve steps, just be sure—again—that you aren't creating a departmental structure where people are hyper-focused on their own step. If people see pricing too early and down the road sales has more than they can handle, ultimately your funnel cracks.

Most people don't have clear visibility into the funnel. It's spread out to different parts of the organization and nobody takes ownership of it. But marketing can play a much stronger role now, in terms of acting like sales—that is, marketing can forecast exactly the way sales can.

It is the marketing department's job now to say, "Based on the amount of interest we have in our product this month, we can make the following predictions." We can tell the sales department to ramp up or down the number of sales agents two weeks or three months from now. This type of forecasting is something every CMO can provide, but most don't. Why not?

Because even though the boundaries between marketing departments and sales teams are dissolving, and even if you are part of a forward-thinking company that is set up for handling measurements—the challenge remains in communicating what those measurements mean to everybody across all departments. And then, of course, all departments have to get their act together in how they respond to those measurements.

So why not let the funnel itself help explain to the rest of the company what's going on in marketing? Show a clear funnel with numbers next to it: "We're generating this amount of interest at this step, and at the next step, this amount." Stop trying to explain marketing with jargon, "365,000 people signed up for our newsletter this month." Nobody outside of marketing knows how that translates.

"I have X amount of people at the top of my funnel today, and I anticipate this amount will come out at the bottom in X amount of time," is all everybody wants to hear. That Pulitzer-worthy newsletter? No offense to writers, but I didn't even read it.

Chapter Seven

Marketing Machines and the Building Blocks of Disruptive Marketing

Keeping Marketing Innovation Real and Practical

Many marketing books pontificate about marketing strategies and results. They provide an overall report on the current "state of marketing" and then lay out what we should do to improve our approach: We need a "better digital approach," or we need to "build an online presence." But for me, it's my job as CMO to get my team thinking about marketing as a machine—to think of this machine as a well-oiled system, a scalable operation.

I then have to help the company or organization I'm working with to see this machine clearly, and set my team to honing in and making it as lean and powerful as possible.

The machine, to me, is everything—all else is just managerial noise.

Not that these books and managerial concerns aren't important—they can be. But at the end of the day I have to ask: How does my machine work better than other companies' machines? How can we improve it? How does my machine address company priorities? It is *the how* I care about more than anything else.

A business can have any number of priorities, and the order of these priorities can change as the company changes—or not. Banks will probably always go for stability. Start-ups will probably always go for growth. The machine you build had better take your company's priorities into account though. If you're weak in customer support, is it a priority to fix that? Telephone companies notoriously do not see customer support as part of their growth. Their main concern is: How do we reduce the cost to our call centers? If each call costs an average of X-dollars and they have a million calls a day, shaving off 10 cents a call results in tremendous savings. Phone companies take the risk they will lose a customer or two when they reach that "last resort"—the call center—but they realize they are better off adding up all those dimes.

In some cases, customer support is the lowest-maintenance building block of the machine; in other cases, the highest-maintenance. Zappos' customer service is a prime example of the latter, where the customer service experience is so uniquely good—that everyone still raves about it. It isn't a stretch to say that Zappos customer service is an important part of their marketing machine. One could even say that they dominate in customer service.

"Market domination" is certainly an exciting term—and it is an exciting goal for a company or for one building block of the machine to reach for, but I tend to think of it as another academic notion that just isn't practical. Old-school theorists love to tout the ability of a company to become Number One, if only the marketing team could figure out how to "bend the will of demand to the will of supply." I confess I don't even know what that really means though. Yes, once in a while someone comes on the scene and becomes known as a market maker—that is, they create a market that didn't exist before, but this is exceptional.

Apple did this, of course. Every marketing book cites them. But consider also, vitamins. Nobody needs vitamins unless they have a specific medical condition, but in the 1940s, vitamin marketers created the need. The vitamin industry is now a 12-billion-dollar a year industry. Shampoo for curly hair is pretty much the same as shampoo for straight hair, but the beauty industry sells most households two bottles of "specialized" shampoo instead of one— plus the two corresponding bottles of conditioner.

This is part of the marketing machine, no doubt: Marketers are supposed to find ways to create needs. Creating a need that consumers didn't know they had is impressive. Bending the curves of supply and demand might be the marketer's Holy Grail. But how about tackling our in-the-trenches challenges in more grounded terms—as I do—via disruption. You disrupt the market when you change perceptions, and in this way, you do create and bend markets.

Lofty marketing goals and abstract marketing concepts are nice to have, but they don't always translate well into actionable tactics, clear objectives, or clear priorities. In fact, they often end up causing more kinks in the machine of bigger organizations, where a lot of reporting ends up sounding like the work of magicians. When I see a company presenting one reality to investors and another to the press, I know as a business leader that the company is not focused on what really matters.

If you are grounded and focused on creating a machine, then you and everyone on your team knows exactly what needs to be done. If you are getting what needs to be done, done—then you don't have to worry about Being Number One, or dominating the market—that kind of thinking is ridiculous anyway, unless you are Number Two—then you might want to go for it.

Set "Becoming Number One" aside, focus on building a machine that produces very high profit margins, and you will outpace your competition. Costco disrupted business-as-usual by building a machine that allowed them to keep costs low and profit margins high. They make very little money off product sales and a lot of money on membership sales. They've built a machine others haven't been able to catch up to.

What building blocks should a CMO have in hand when putting together the type of machine that leaves others in the dust? Obviously, you need the product itself, advertising, and media acquisition. You need sales, customers, and customer support. Online or offline, you need the teller, the cashier, or the checkout point. You need returns and any materials that come with the product, such as manuals, technical instructions, and knowledge bases.

Sometimes too, you set out all your building blocks, place them in a sequence that aligns with your priorities, build your machine, and everything is going well enough—but then the unexpected amazing happens. Take Ikea's assembly instructions: I doubt anyone at Ikea originally thought of them as even a minor building block, but people talk about Ikea instructions—Ikea instructions are a thing. They have become, in effect, a part of Ikea's marketing machine.

Product packaging is another critical building block of the machine for many industries—it's obvious with those curly versus straight hair shampoo bottles, but what about lumber?

For the longest time, bundles of lumber would arrive at construction sites, and nobody could tell one batch of lumber from that of the competitor's—until... one of the smaller lumber suppliers figured out a way to leverage free advertising space by putting huge stamps on their batches. Sure, this lumber would end up hidden behind the walls of houses, but on the way to the site and while sitting on-site, the brand name was getting out there. If you are a lumberyard, do you consider your delivery trucks only as pieces of logistical equipment? If you are the CMO, you need to consider them as a marketing asset—they are a building block in your marketing machine.

Of course, the largest building block of any machine is usually the service or product itself, and you can make this product free, half free, or "near a product that is free." Starbucks, what do they offer for free? Clean bathrooms. The bathrooms in Starbucks are a great marketing mechanism, because for every person who enters the establishment just to use the bathroom and leave, another person feels guilty and purchases a latte. There is no obligation to make a purchase, but even if just five percent of people who use the bathroom at Starbucks end up buying a coffee, it is well worth paying to have them cleaned. Starbucks essentially adopted a freemium model for their bathrooms: The bathrooms, not just their coffee cups, are a building block in their marketing machine.

So you have your basic building blocks lined up—now how do you resist lining them up like everyone else does?

Hint: No Copycatting!

TripAdvisor arranged its building blocks in a different sequence than its competitors—they did things entirely backwards, in fact—and they continue to score very nicely. Normally, in the online airline ticket market, people are pushed as quickly as possible to checkout, where they might do some quick comparison shopping. When Trip Advisor came along, they decided to take customers through a much longer process, where they would read reviews first, and then purchase their trip. Trip Advisor is proof you can order your building blocks any way you want, and the fact that everyone else is ordering their blocks a different way, is in fact, an opportunity.

Another opportunity is to look at an industry or a company's weakest links. If you're working for an industry that has an abysmal customer service reputation, how can you strengthen this link in your machine —what might happen if you put the customer service block front and center?

One of the first projects I worked on involved precisely this kind of opportunity, and it was in the second-toughest industry in the world to compete in—construction. When people want to redo their kitchen, they think their architect or designer is fabulous, but contractors are all the same. Contractors deliver wildly different prices, but not for one second does anybody think that the price difference actually reflects a difference in quality. Not for one second does anyone believe either that the project will end up costing exactly what the contractor estimates—in fact, we believe it'll be double. Fighting this perception is a challenge for the contractor, who is trying to prove that he can provide quality work and unique craftsmanship in a market where the consumer doesn't think the same way he does.

What is a contractor to do? He walks in and the customer says, "How much is it going to cost?" The contractor says, "Wait. We don't have any specifications yet." The customer says, "I know, but I want to know how much this is going to cost me."

The contractor gives them a price that includes so many stipulations that it's almost random, but ultimately, he is trying to educate people on why he is the most qualified for the job—and either gets the contract or doesn't, based on who else is bidding. Contractors are not the ones in control of the process and they have no way to distinguish themselves from the competition.

My job was to crack the contractor's standard operating procedure via disruptive marketing, and because I realized that one of the main customer concerns at the early stages of the process was cost, I found a way to sum up the entire cost of a project before the contractor even knew what he was going to build. When everybody said it couldn't be done, I replied, "I don't believe that."

Here is what the contractors of this company were then able to do: They went to the customer's home, asked what the customer wanted to achieve, took a couple measurements, and within a few minutes, presented an accurate price on the spot. In addition, they could guarantee at that meeting that the price would never change, unless the scope of the project changed completely.

Success!

Customers get frustrated with what they perceive to be arbitrary pricing and crooked contractors—most of us know this, because we have been these customers. So, while other contracting firms had three meetings with the client before providing a quote, we were able to provide a reliable one on the very first meeting. Imagine that!

And then I said: Let's take this even further. Let's give clients a 3-D rendering of what their new kitchen is going to look like, right there on the spot, in an effort to remove any objections to closing the deal pronto. Let's get them to sign a contract right there at Meeting One!

What did we need to do to make the impossible happen? How were we going to get away with this kind of disruption? It took research and the creation of software. It took creating custom samples and accepting certain risks. The goal was, by the way, to create a very high profit margin. We did it all. We went to 45% percent gross profit in an industry where that number is practically unheard of, and sold the company shortly after.

I might have gotten the idea of flipping an industry's reputation on its head from a company that blew my mind years back. One day, our usual plumber couldn't make it, so unfortunately for him, I stumbled upon Rodenheiser Plumbing.

Plumbing is a messy job. The standard expectation is that somebody's going to come into your home, sum up your problem, estimate hours and parts—and then go way over budget. And there is nothing you can do about it.

But what happened with Rodenheiser? A nice guy in a beautiful clean suit showed up in a very modern oversized van, at exactly the time he said he would. After introducing himself, he pulled some boot covers over his shoes, took a look at our water pump, walked back out to his vehicle, and presented me with a beautifully-bound book of plumbing parts and equipment. He turned to a page, pointed to a picture of a pump and said, "Here's what you need."

There was a price next to to the photo, of $365.

I said, "That's impressive. How much will labor be?"

He said, "Oh no, that's $365 total. Labor is included in the price of the pump."

I was astounded, and then he told me he wasn't leaving to go to Home Depot to search for the right items. I signed and paid, and within a half hour, the pump arrived via truck and the work was done shortly after.

Rodenheiser Plumbing operated in a way that I like to operate now—they asked what the complete opposite of doing business would look like, and in their case, they built a machine with a digitally connected warehouse where they knew exactly what parts they had and where they were located. They printed up beautifully bound books that showed total pricing. Everything was highly organized and scaled up—at the time, they had over a dozen trucks.

In my mind, the company re-imagined how to fit their building blocks together. They said: Customer satisfaction is pretty damn low in plumbing, so let's bring it to the top. I haven't stopped telling the Rodenheiser story. They changed everything; they reshuffled the pieces.

I remember standing in my driveway as the man in the clean suit and fancy van backed out, thinking, "If this kind of machine can be built in the plumbing industry, imagine the possibilities."

It also struck me that the worse the public perception, the more the industry suffers from a bad name, the more of an opportunity you have to disrupt.

Imagine the possibilities. Then build your machine.

Chapter Eight

The Very Top of the Funnel

Where Quality Might Matter More than One Might Think

All of us can call to mind one of those weird business locations where no matter who moves in and sets up shop, they just don't make it. "That place used to be a restaurant," you say, "then it was a shoe store, after that it was a tattoo shop."

Whatever it was, it could never manage to generate traffic.

Traditionally, if you chose a lousy location, odds were you were doomed. Traditionally then, in terms of generating traffic, location mattered, as did word of mouth and placing the biggest ads and most ads in the papers.

In essence, not much has changed: Sure, we now have social and more channels are available to small businesses that weren't available to your Mom and Pop stores. But from what I've seen lately, traffic generation strategies are in many ways shifting in reverse gear, because the rules in the digital marketplace are (re)evolving straight back to a pay-to-play field.

In the early days of the Internet and E-commerce, and up to just a few years ago, you could put up your app on an app store, and chances were it would get downloaded—there just weren't that many apps around. Or, you could count on your website or blog to generate traffic, simply because it existed. It's hard to recall, but for a long while, competition really was that slim.

Now, everybody's got an app, a blog, a website, and social, so: Whoever has more resources is going to float to the top and be seen more often, by more people. That is, although technically the playing field for getting an interview with Oprah without paying for it is equal, everybody and their mother wants their O-moment, and so at the end of the day it's mostly a pay-to-play (or pay to make the top-echelon, life-altering radar) arena.

So, here we marketers are full-circle, still trying to figure out how we can get customers to notice us. It has always been—and still is—very difficult. Back in the day, you could place ads, and do direct mail and email. We still do all this, and we hustle with the new stuff too.

The central difference that digital has introduced is this: In 1999, if you sent out direct mail and somebody showed up in your store the next day, you didn't know and didn't think you could know what percentage of your direct mail actually was working. Unless you were conducting extensive and very expensive audits, you could not quantify the impact of your direct mail campaign, and therefore could not continually adjust and refine it. You had no systematic way of testing and comparing variations of your direct mail messages or offers—so you kept mailing away.

Technology changed everything.

Now you can measure the effectiveness of your direct mail or radio ad campaign with something as simple as a coupon code. Notice that the bulk of your newest customers are entering the code "Wait, Wait, Don't Tell Me," and you have a signal! You've got NPR fans. You can work these signals on and offline. The critical thing now is how you handle your incoming data. That is, now as more data comes in, you have to pick and choose which packets of data you're going to deal with. You have to get systematic about your systems.

Most of us know this, but I still see too many people making the mistake of saying: "We've got our Facebook page and two of our content people are graduates of the SEO Ivy Leagues! We've got an Etsy page and Twitter. So hey, we're marketing!"

Setting up all the smashing social and SEO in the world and compiling data though is not the same as creating actual and meaningful awareness. Data can and will help you determine what resonates, but before you can even begin to acquire data, your company has to know deep in its own bones what it stands for.

And still, again, I've had CEOs tell me, "Just make sure everybody knows about us."

But what is the point of people knowing that you exist? If they don't know what benefit you bring to the world, or more specifically, what benefit you bring to them, they will not pursue you. The fact that somebody has been exposed to your product doesn't mean they understand it. Maybe they were attracted by your snazzy logo—but if they can't quickly grasp your relevance, they will move on to the next thing that not only catches their eye, but that connects with them in some vital way.

The best marketers understand that creating awareness entails standing for a cause or a value. You can be a rocking company on the brink of rock star status, but if your audience cannot tie your message to what matters, forget it! Rackspace might have found a way to generate more awareness, for example, when they brought onboard social media and tech evangelist Robert Scoble, but while Scoble certainly put Rackspace's name on the map (finally), does anyone really know what they stand for? And why does Amazon consistently kick Rackspace's butt?

(It's hard to answer that first question, but to the second question, I say: Amazon is agnostic. They'll host anything, they're scalable, and they are the cheapest option out there.) I know a lot about amazon's USP, but I haven't got a clue about what Rackspace's is, even if I did run into Scoble on social every other day.

So, Rackspace might once have been a potential leader in its market, and Scoble certainly gave his brilliant best to create awareness, but they're still way behind and now Scoble has moved on. (This is not to say that Scoble is no good. He is frankly, an amazing social influencer, but the program did not take advantage of his clout).

Building awareness based on the mindset: "Just get us in front of people," is not only costly, it's worthless.

The other huge mistake marketing departments make in terms of generating awareness is not thinking carefully enough about who they want to attract. Who is your potential customer? A lot of newer companies set unrealistic expectations in this regard: We want to be a household name! First of all, you can't become a household name—you need to become a brand. Secondly, there is almost no chance you can become a brand in the next ten years, unless you are in a very niche market.

It's important then, not to spread your efforts too thinly. Does your neighbor across the street need to know about your business? Will it benefit you if they do? Chances are, no. If they do know, it means that, weather you know it or not, you are investing money and effort in them. Does the grocer next door or the Pizza Hut need to know about your business? No, not unless you're selling pepperoni. Before you declare you want your pepperoni to be a household name, pick apart all possible audiences, and then go narrow and go deep.

Focusing makes you instantly more effective: X, Y, and Z are the people that are going to potentially buy from you. Out of the starting gates, you leverage the critical mass effect of X, Y, and Z by forgetting about A, B, and C! Think about it: If your message is spread over too wide an audience, a billion people may hear about you, but they'll hear about you once and that's it—your message will die away in the noise.

You need to hit people many times with a message before they will come visit you—even for the first time. Once they visit, it may take a dozen more visits before they take action. These are tough stats to swallow, but you can start to sway these stats in your favor by aiming for a very targeted audience: "Let's find doctors in Boston proper."

"Okay, what kind of doctors?"

Marketing success bleeds out. Chances are that if you have decided to deeply target pediatricians in Boston, you'll start to see pediatricians from New York and Chicago sniffing around. Your best campaigns are organic, they breathe and take on a life of their own. The better you can track your next target group's next inhale, the faster you can ride out the exhale of the target group you just conquered, and be there at the exact moment your "next up" needs you.

Focus first on winning your Boston pediatricians well, then win them in NYC, and then in Chicago. There is no race to become a household name overnight. It may look like the giants did that, but most of them did not. I've said it once and I'll say it a thousand times—which in itself sounds antiquated, but I don't care—hard work is the only way to achieve marketing success. We live in quick times, but there is still no get-rich-quick marketing solution, so put your hard hat on and prepare to take on a small community and attack them from all directions.

Now, what if you have this great product and this great content and all of a sudden, say you are a plumbing company in Los Angeles, you see: "Shazam! We've had 1000% increase in visitors. What does this mean? Our content is so good that we're reaching people in Dubai."

That's not going to benefit you at all. Or is it?

Well, yes and no. No, because in business, you never just add value to the world. Banks will donate money to a concert hall or medical cause, but it's not because they're performing a good deed—it's in their marketing budget. The question really is, "Okay, I've spent money, time, and effort, and people are showing up to my site that obviously are never going to be my actual customers. What do I need to figure out?"

Ask yourself first: What have I done? Am I attracting the wrong audience or is this just a byproduct of having a powerful message? As CMO, I always assume we will attract mostly the right audience, but will also inevitably attract some of the wrong audience. That's part of the cost of doing business. Even if you figure out how to hone in as tightly as possible on your target, you'll still bring in outliers. You then can do one of two things: You can ignore them, or you can figure out a value to gain out of them.

For instance, maybe for the local plumber in L.A., the job of the interested parties in Dubai is to boost his SEO, or to share his content on social. Maybe their job is to comment on his blog: "This information is wonderful. Thank you."

There are multiple creative ways to derive value from interested parties, the challenge is to determine which ways are worth it, and how. At Roojoom, for example, we found that teachers love our product. Though most of us are huge fans of education—how could you not be?—right now we have no plans to monetize this sector. As a business, education provides us no value, so in terms of marketing, we don't offer a freemium version to educators.

Instead, we offer them our product in exchange for quality assurance. Because Roojoom has a few clients that pay a lot of money for our product, rather than a lot of clients that pay a little, we need more massive traffic to use our system so we can test it. We give teachers a watered-down version of our system for free, and they find and report bugs before our paying customers do. Voila! We have found a way of extracting value from an audience we weren't quite sure what to do with at first glance.

Always take that second glance!

That said, if you are an advertising-heavy business, where most of your model is built around traffic acquisition and you are attracting people from Istanbul when you're in Tallahassee, you're buying the wrong traffic. This illustrates what I mentioned earlier: You don't want people in Istanbul to even know you exist. It's just too damn expensive.

Here we are talking about traffic generation as an organic mechanism, one that bleeds out, one that inhales and exhales—if we're good at it. But what's the nitty gritty: What are the five concrete ways to generate traffic?

The simplest categories are paid-for traffic; word of mouth; social, which consists of a combination of paid-for and free; guest posting on blogs, which I sometimes refer to as Poor Man's PR, or "showing up in different places online," (and which is sometimes seen as part of content marketing, but is not); influencer marketing; and SEO.

The science of SEO has been figured out: You optimize your content, try to get people to talk about you, and try to steer good websites to refer to you. SEO has become a very technical task. Some people will overpay an agency to do it, but it's pretty straightforward. Your marketing department can fit it into their methodology, and before posting anything, skim it, make changes, and go for it.

PR nowadays too, is pretty simple. If you can generate news, then you can do PR. You can contact the media. Of course, let's face it, most of us are not newsworthy—most companies are not newsworthy. But, if we have enough budget and the right company culture, we can create news. Or, we can just "show up in more places online," by mapping out the influential places, starting with the low-hanging fruit and moving up. That's right, guest blog—show up in front of your audiences in the right places, and garner those third-party recommendations.

Too many companies think too little of the power of third-party recommendations, but they carry a lot of weight and aren't that hard to generate. If you're selling sparkly swively dental chairs, for example, be where dentists read online. As for a print target, *Dentistry Tools Today* will be more valuable to you than a spot in the *New York Times*. This should be evident, but I can't tell you how many CEOs I've heard tout the importance of a placement in the "big" magazines, even though they'd reach many more potential customers for a lot fewer dollars if they just gave it five minutes thought. There are, of course, other reasons a company might want to be in the mainstream news—investor relations, employee pride, recruiting power, and so on—but, in general, these are not the marketer's concerns..

Finally, under the umbrella of PR, we can "do something crazy." This might entail anything from enlisting the help of Improv Everywhere, to suing each other a lot—like Apple and Samsung do. What gets you talked about or in the news, and what are you willing to spend or do for that coverage, is up to you.

On the more practical end of things—for most companies—there's social media and its very close sister, word-of-mouth. Social waxes and wanes in popularity, but at this point it's safe to say that it is never going to go away completely. Currently, we look at channels like Periscope, Snapchat, and WhatsApp, and we don't know quite what to do with it all. How, as a company, do I use WhatsApp for generating traffic? And what about Snapchat, where everything is simply about the here-and-now? How do you market in that world? If you know, please email me the answer. I confess I don't have a solid one right now.

Still, we try. We have no choice but to accept all the new social that makes even the thirty-somethings on our team feel ancient, because the promise and thrill behind social is if you get it right and if you're lucky and if you systematically work at it, you can go viral. Or, if you can create the kind of post that for every dollar you put into it brings you six shares in addition to a certain percentage of clicks, you are golden.

Social provides social proof: Our audience wants to know that they are not the only person that's making this decision, even a small one, such as "liking" a post. Social gives us a huge window and at the same time provides a sense of security. Awareness is created via social, for sure, but so too is traffic generation when people see conversations taking place about your products.

Whether going viral is somewhat based on luck or is a combination of luck and science, it can be done in many ways. It can be done organically, or sort of "spammingly," where you as CMO put out the mandate: "Okay, let's just post like crazy," which I have often had my staff do, daily, with a little help from our social-automation platform.

It should be a requirement that employees in all departments of a company help spread the good word—evangelize—this I believe, because the divide between the personal brand and the corporate brand is eroding. The heavily-PR-backed corporate brand reeks of smoke and mirrors. We inhabit now instead, a social environment, where people want to hear from their friends.

Ultimately and ideally, some traffic generation is going to be out of your hands—rejoice! Let anybody anywhere in the company further your cause on social. As CMO, use your influence inside your company to build structures that leverage social to the max. Encourage everyone to share often, consistently, actively, and authentically.

And do not forget, alongside the new and mysterious social media, you have the old standby: media buying. Media buying is very quantitative, very performance based, and very fast-paced. These days, much of it is managed by computers, or by what is called programmatic advertising.

Basically, we give Google or Facebook or some other system a chunk of money and say, "You know how to spend this better than I do. Go ahead." We let the algorithms figure out in real-time, "Does X increase my price-per-click? Let's shift the money to Y then. How does that compare? Better? Let's keep our money with Y."

Media buying is very powerful, but requires a flawless analytic system to leverage it fully. Everything has to be ship shape in terms of tracking and cookies and all the beautiful geeky stuff. What becomes most interesting in media buying is merging the geekery with the message you want to put out there.

You can never forget, no matter what mix of strategies and tactics you are using, that consumers are moving away from anything that hints at corporate vacuity, and are all about leaping onto the bandwagon—as long as their friends are there and they can gather some sense of meaning and value.

As CMO, I am always asking my marketing team, "The data is good, these numbers and percentages are great, so how can we continue to create a better experience? And how in the age of Snapchat, can we still build something that lasts?"

Acquiring traffic can be easily scaled (with the proper staff and budget), but to properly scale you have to make sure you have the technology in place to tag every individual you lure in to your funnel. Doing this will allow you to analyze the funnel for every channel, every segment and every source, and cross reference that channel's performance against its costs.

Chapter Nine

Keeping Your Audiences Interested

Managing the Customer's Emotional Journey

A company has to be in very bad shape, like Macy's has been in recent years, to get internal buy-in on a complete overhaul. In most cases, rather than swapping out everything you do and stand for in order to generate more interest and become the next "Apple of Retail," you're going to root for and succeed with little wins. You'll aim to be all-out disruptive with one content hub or one store location, or even with one blog post, one ad, or one case study.

For example, most marketers present their case studies and at the end pose the question: Want to learn more? They collect the customer's information then. But what if we did it the other way around? What might happen if we asked the people cruising our site for their information before they got the case study? Let's gate our content—or some of it—earlier than usual and test if that works to generate more interest. Why not? Because standard practice says otherwise, but being different is your chance to be disruptive, even in the little things… particularly in the little things.

> Generating interest sometimes means simply doing things differently than others. That could mean have a unique product or just a very unique website. Remember: playing it safe means you are inherently less interesting.

The fact is, interest generation is the Number One challenge for most marketers. Everyone writes about it and holds hours-long meetings about it, but nobody has a clue what they're doing. It's like a first date, but worse—it's a pre-date. The most powerful algorithms in the world might be running dating sites like eHarmony, but how many people never make it past the first email exchange to a first coffee?

Interest is undeniably a tough nut to crack, but still, somebody is always giving us a product or an industry and telling us: Work with it. Make everyone want it.

Ninety-nine percent of the time, the products and the services we are given though, are very similar to everything else. That's the stark reality. Out of desperation, many marketers will opt for brute force in order to rise above the fray—they'll repeat the same thing over and over, but with slight variations. They'll send emails: "Hey! I saw you are interested. When can I speak to you next week to discuss benefits?"

But let's be honest: Half the time nobody cares, or rather, they understand that even your interest and enthusiasm over the plastic dinnerware you are selling is entirely fabricated. Only a contractor is in love with a 2-by-4, and nobody is in love with toothpaste, not even dentists. No matter what you are marketing, you have to find a way to reach beyond "love" of your product; you have to surround it with an interesting story.

Interesting stories attract and hold interest. Of course, story creation takes talent, a healthy budget, and most importantly, time. SEO is useful, but if you don't have someone on your team who can link key words together into amazing sentences that thrum through space and wrap around potential customers' emotions like ivy vines around trellis—or that pierce into potential customers' emotions like thorns—okay, you get where I'm going with this. Marketers tend magical content gardens. Fill these gardens with sweet roses, or with plain old iceberg lettuce, or with stinging nettles—but mix it up, make it vibrant, bring the buzzing bees! And then nurture and prune the ingredients you believe will get under your customers' skin.

Recognize and accept the fact that there is no KPI for emotion, then get down to the business of finding a way to make your messages impact lives. Generate interest by taking people on a journey through your material. Work on flow.

Shooting out emails and five blog posts a day will often create an effect or reaction that is the opposite of flow. If the marketing team has clearly made no attempt to meet me on an emotional level, they are essentially pushing me to unsubscribe. We all get too much clutter. Only the striking material is given the privilege of remaining.

Even in the B2B world, we are finally recognizing—emotion counts. No matter the product, we are still marketing to people. Initial intrigue, desire, excitement—it's all a form of capital and if you strike at the right moment, it will be easier to prompt that person to buy impulsively or to share your story. Hook them and then make an offer for 30% off now, 50% off next purchase, or delivery tomorrow—but remember, beyond a great deal, you can only keep them hooked via their emotions. Macy's learned this the hard way when they eliminated sales events and just offered consistent bargain prices. Logically, your customer base may know your profits are six in one hand, half a dozen in the other, but if "special" sales events twelve times a year make them more excited than lower prices every single week of every single month of the year, they'll be disappointed and will seek that magic "sale aura" elsewhere.

Is there a way to systemize emotions, or manage them? I don't think so. That's the beauty of human emotion, and the challenge of it for us as marketers. Live with it. The best I can offer is this: You'll know emotionally compelling marketing material when you see it.

I know, I'm sorry. You might have come to this chapter seeking clear guidelines on generating interest, but you might as well try to explain why two people who have been married for thirty-five years suddenly call it quits with no reason other than: We fell out of love.

Emotion is challenging to dissect and fabricate, but it does help if everyone working on your team and working for your company is emotionally engaged on one level or another, with what you are trying to bring to your targeted customers. So you see, there are no guidelines—just the somewhat clichéd truth: Love what you do and hope it seeps through and bleeds out and infuses into the bloodstream of your customers.

Gardens and infusions? I'm suddenly sounding like a bad poet here.

Let's talk about toilet paper.

How in the hell does as a toilet paper manufacturer pretend to love their product? How do they emote about it, without turning all their lunch guests off entirely: "Oh, the 2-ply structure really makes the wiping experience…" CUT!

Right?

One company, Angel Soft, did their toilet paper campaign right. Dare I say, they did something beautiful! Rather than drone on and on about their product's softer or thicker features, they connected with toilet paper users (99.9% of the modern world), emotionally. They created a tribute to all fathers who were single dads, who were having a hard time doing it all alone—wherein they communicated that the one thing these overworked doting dads could trust was their toilet paper. We know that most of us will never fall in love with one toilet paper brand over the other, and that we talk about ads that are about "everything but the product itself," i.e. sex sells (maybe not toilet paper—but maybe)! After that Fathers' Day toilet paper ad ran, maybe audiences at least smiled, appreciated the effort, and picked that brand up their next time out.

Stories that connect with people encourage them, literally, to connect with your product.

With emotion in mind then, and with high hopes at connecting with it, I think what works is to identify touchpoints, then strike. If somebody just signed up for newsletter, that's not a meaningful touchpoint, but if they expressed interest in my product and are waiting for something amazing, I can now ask them for something in return. If I am a fun spirited car company for example, I can give my potential customers the tools to build their own unique car—they can add a single-flower vase to their dashboard. Once a customer has created their vehicle, they're excited. Now is the time to strike—I cannot let them close this page! If they won't enter their information into a form so that a salesperson can contact them, or won't actually buy a car this weekend, maybe I can at least get them to share with their 3,500 Facebook friends the fabulous car they just spent half-an-hour creating. It's amazing to me how few automotive brands get this. For some of us, car buying is the largest emotional purchase of our lifetime, but there is nothing emotional in the customer journey. Or at least nothing WAS emotional, until Tesla came along and opened up showrooms in malls next to Neiman-Marcus. Talk about smart one-stop luxury shopping!

Marketing relevant touchpoints can occur too, on the other end of the spectrum: Customers call support when they're distressed. This is a great time to capitalize. Take advantage of their distress and nip it in the bud by employing the martial arts technique of swinging your customers' energy around to turn things to your favor. Delight! Smooth the bumpy ride! Provide a great soundtrack.

Just recognize that the time to ask somebody for something is when they're emotional. This is true of all people, regardless of age or generation—and in fact, in my opinion, many of those Gen-labels are meaningless. What counts more is shared common interests: How do I get to soccer fans on an emotional level? Soccer fans of eighty are likely to have more in common with soccer fans of twenty than they are to have with polo players of eighty—when it comes to what makes them tick. What makes them soccer fans spend hundreds of dollars on jerseys and scarves and flags?

You can cut the marketing matrix in so many ways: You can focus primarily on generation X, Y, or Z, and yes of course, they are as different from each other as they are from the Greatest Generation. But what is most interesting to me when it comes to creating content that will grab people on an emotional level, is voice and tone. Are you kind of wacky, geeky, or overly serious? Good, now put all your passion behind what you are and what you are doing and hire a specialist, or versatile constant learner. Aim for authenticity by taking the time first to determine what your company, product, service, and employees stand for—then hone in and take it all to the extreme.

Smoke and mirrors have changed. Nobody falls for the same kind of gimmicks we used to—but we still fall. Marketing is a game, and while you never want to toy with your customers' emotions, every single one of us understands that we are playing and are being played. We have built-in learning mechanisms where we learn to trust certain signals and to distrust others, and once we learn these signals, it is very hard to change them. But we eventually do, and we evolve.

For instance, in the 1950s, we "knew better" than to buy anything made in Japan. The United States made better stuff. Forty years later, Sony blew our minds. Several years ago, the public decided "Let's not trust brands; let's trust outsider sources—like reviews." On Amazon, people began to buy products based on customer reviews, until BAMMO! Everyone started to realize a new game was at play and there were new rules—there was a system of suspect or fake reviews. The cycle that took us from not trusting Japanese products to eating them up lasted fifty years; the cycle from trust to distrust of Amazon reviews took us two.

Cycles are ever-shifting, and are more rapidly shifting than before. So although customers are much more skeptical and much more informed—they no longer trust what brands tell them as much as what their friends report—we are all still fundamentally incapable of making our own decisions. The marketer relies on discovering and leveraging this sweet spot: The marketer aims between the armor of distrust, skepticism, and too much knowledge, to where the emotional human resides, to where we all sit looking in the mirror and wondering, "What do I need to buy and possess in order to become more intelligent, efficient, attractive, successful, popular, and content?"

It is the marketer's job to think through an entire storyline for consumers. Tweets are powerful and marketers have used them in very creative ways, but a story is not written for a quick win. A solid story has the power to keep consumers engaged in one realm, one community, one topic so that they don't just stay a short time, but feel so comfortable they never want to leave—they never want to explore the competition.

Building this type of ecosystem takes vision. It takes picturing what a long walk side-by-side with customer will look like. How will you build interest and trust initially, and how will you maintain it? If marketers started to think about their relationship to the customer as one as serious, as complex, and as challenging as a long-term friendship or marriage—we might be closer to being onto something.

You have those friends you know want a divorce. The wife tells your wife about it; the husband tells you—but they don't split, and won't ever, because it is in our DNA not to break our emotional connections. Emotion is an investment.

As marketers, we may never be able to demystify the multivariate components of human emotion, but we can ready ourselves for those crucial fate-deciding moments of truth: We can have the breath mint in our pocket, or already in our mouth, when we walk with our date to the front door of our building.

In the end, we all want that kiss. That kiss signifies that we are attractive and trustworthy, and that perhaps a future committed relationship is possible. We all want to be the "hero" in our own story, but the truth is, is that every great story we have ever heard is a version of the exact same one: Hero enters "game," faces challenges, questions his/her ability to overcome challenges, meets mentor, gets the golden key (which he/she has always possessed), and thrives.

That is to say, we know how every story goes, so it is the marketer's job to be the Yoda.

If we can help bring consumers to their decision, as they are discovering their powers and offering up some sort of sacrifice, it's a win-win story. Luke Skywalker becomes the hero—in part because Yoda said, "Trust in yourself." He generated interest by getting Luke interested in his own ability to master the Force. Mentor hooked student.

Pick (the) one powerful story, then adjust the voice and tone to your specific product, service, or brand. Integrate what you stand for into your marketer-as-mentor role, and rather than throwing out a bunch of meaningless random communications, take people on a journey. Whether you are selling razors, adult diapers, or oil gaskets, remember that at the end of the day, the customer wants to be a hero, the customer wants a happy ending.

Create incremental expectations—or mircromoments—build gates and open them—provide the promise that something better is always around the corner. Don't be boring.

> Dollar Shave Club did not succeed by creating a new, better, more interesting razor. They did it solely by creating a new, better, more interesting voice and tone.

There's a lot of talk in psychological circles about the value of "closure," but in marketing circles, if there is just one thing we know about interest generation, it is that the open-ended drive-people-crazy quest to be more of something keeps interest alive.

Chapter Ten

Rope Like a Girl

The Seductive Art of Lead Generation and Conversion

Google the word "conversion" and you'll come up with pages of lists of the top five tactics, the top ten, and even the top six-hundred and sixty-six (in which some funny marketer compiled a bunch of top five, ten, and twenty lists).

Clearly, everyone believes they are an expert on conversion, or they hope if you throw a list of their tricks at your conversion problems, everything will work out, and you will Tweet their praises. But what does conversion really mean?

Conversion means different things to different people. For the marketer, conversion means moving customers from one stage of the funnel to another. In sales, conversion means a sale. In B2B, conversion is typically done on the phone or in the mail. Typically in e-Commerce, it is done completely digitally online. Technically speaking, conversion can also happen simply when somebody clicks a button, or it can happen in a separate system on a separate website, where essentially that database then reports to another database.

What's important when talking about conversion then, is first, recognizing that it means different things to different people in different departments, and second, that you have to keep your conversion tactics consistent with your growth and pricing models. Though a quick search on Google might lead you to believe that conversion in the marketer's Holy Grail, unfortunately, it is not. If you talk to somebody who is in email marketing, their Holy Grail is click-through. As far as they are concerned, the click-through ratio on their email is conversion. They are obsessed with how many people or what percentage of people are clicking. These people probably dance to a soundtrack of clicks in their dreams every night.

Somebody clicking through an email though, is equivalent to somebody clicking through one page of your website to another. It can be completely meaningless. Modern marketers work backwards from the conversion, starting with the question: "What series of steps does a person take to get to the conversion?" or "How do I move more people from one place to another until they reach that spot?" This is the best way to do it, but the problem with taking this backwards approach is that it doesn't always reflect and respect the reality of the model a company is using, or the expectations a company has set up.

For example, again, the number and the type of steps between traffic and interest generation, and conversion, varies between models. Sales in a B2B environment is handled by the sales department, rather than by funneling leads through the product. Also, when marketing says, "Hey, I gave you the lead but you didn't close it, what happened?" sales comes back with "The leads you gave me were bad," and animosity grows.

More importantly, this simple point is often missed: At the end of the day, marketers care more about generating leads than they do about conversion, because lead generation is how their success is measured.

So, the marketer thinks she is solid and respectable when she can say to sales, "I have a 1000 leads a month I'm going to give you." But what if sales can only handle 100 leads? Alright, they'll be scrambling to pick the top of the crop, but how do they begin to measure that? How do they determine out of the 1000 leads they've just been handed which 100 are *most* ready to purchase, most capable of purchasing, and most in need of the product?

The challenge then, in the midst of all the conversion micro-optimizations being pushed at us 24/7 (use green buttons instead of red and make sure all your testimonials are accompanied by client head shots) is that we need to make sure the leads we are handing off, whether 25 or 2500, are solid. We have checked them out in the CRM, and know they are ready to convert.

> Every time a lead gets handed from one department to the next, the chance of it dropping out of the funnel doubles.

Nowadays, you do see marketing and sales working more frequently hand-in-hand, first doing a product demo and then following up with a sale. You can't go wrong building this relationship, and we even have begun to refer to this alliance as "smarketing." Think about it: Hand-offs have a higher chance of turning into true conversions if the marketer is able to tell a sales counterpart, "I nurtured this lead, and I know they're ready for you," rather than offering a simple, "Hey here's a list of leads, take them and go!"

So, forget those promises that changing the color of a button or the layout of your homepage will increase your conversions by 600%. For most companies, most of the time, most of these micro-optimizations are bogus and should be completely ignored.

What matters when it comes to conversion, is ease of conversion: That is, the more friction you put behind the shopping experience, the fewer people will shop. If you give people the option to think twice about the commitment they are about to make, they will think twice.

Gear your funnel for flow. Even if you aren't moving volumes of customers through like Amazon or eBay (and most of us aren't), ask yourself how much time you might potentially waste tweaking and re-tweaking all the thousand little things the thousands of articles are insisting we should all be tweaking. Then ask how much you might gain by doing these tweaks? If your answer is "Another $500 per week," stop obsessing and get back to the hard work I keep insisting is necessary in marketing.

Stop obsessively reading and sharing social media on the value of reading and sharing social media.

Yes, as marketers, educating ourselves and staying current is critical, but there's a limit. Stay smart on the big picture, and the little picture items will fall into line. If you think you are going to miraculously do 1000 times better than your competition by having better stock photos, please take a vacation in one of those places you see in stock photos.

If you are Amazon or eBay, then tweaking something that brings you a half-a-percentage or even one-tenth of a percent increase in your conversion rate, yes—that can add up to a tremendous amount of money. These companies are in the minority though, in that they can afford to hire an entire floor of people whose job it is to sit all day and tweak out! So stop stressing. You and your competition most likely cannot afford one spare person for all the micro-tweaks you're imagining you need.

For most start-ups and "average-sized" businesses, as long as you focus on creating content that connects with people's emotions— you can create an experience that is conducive to shopping. I'm not going to say, "It's that simple," because in the last chapter I admitted that creating great content is an insanely challenging task. But let's just say: Marry your emotionally-geared content with some conversion-inducing "buttons, visuals, and testimonials" and create forms where the customer is not asked to give up his or her firstborn, and you are probably good enough to go!

And go you must! Let go and ignore the constant static about all the magic potions that might bring you a half-a-percentage higher CTR. Do you want to be a solid marketer in terms of conversion? Then focus on creating a seamless customer experience.

Take Etsy for example—Etsy provides a great experience for people who are looking for boutiquish, artsy, homemade stuff. They are consistent, and if they ever went nuts and decided to overhaul their shopping experience to look like some B2B site, they would die within a month. Again, it's not the little things that matter, it's the big things. Most of the time companies that are having conversion challenges are trying to convert people who are not going to buy from them anyway. A lot of the literature preys on small business and companies that are suffering a certain pain level because they don't sell enough. "What's the quick fix?" these companies are asking. "Where's the magic portion?" There is none—it's all click bait!

The basic principle is simple: Come in with a promise and if the promise is interesting, people will consider buying your product. Now, people are always skeptical and it is the customer's job to do their due diligence. They all must maintain a certain level of skepticism by default. Customers compare prices or do research before actually hitting the Buy Now button. The higher the price tag, the more due diligence they feel they need to make. Does the decision they make depend on how fantastic your stock photos are? Really?

Maybe yes, and maybe no, but the bottom line is that people know a reputable site when they see it. In this day and age, while one red button may or may not make or break you, just remember: Don't look cheap. Don't look sleazy. There you go—there are my "top two tips for conversion."

Do testimonials help you look more reputable? Often times they do, but they are not mandatory. Consider Starbucks: They don't need testimonials. Their product has been there forever and you can find proof that their coffee is popular on Every Corner, USA. If you aren't Starbucks however, and the market research you have done reveals that people saying, "Hmm, okay, your product looks good, but…" it is your job to answer the following: "What are people skeptical about, and how do we quell their doubts?"

Figure out how to reduce your customers' objections and give them as few reasons as possible to reconsider hitting Buy Now, and you are on your way to succeeding. Do not stop in your efforts to relieve people of their skepticism: Make it your goal to lighten their load so that even if they are online shopping from home in their pajamas, they are made to feel even more comfortable by the sight of your website. Do the images align with your message, product, and story? That in itself is comforting.

Comfort and consistency are critical to attracting and converting consumers. If a template website is inappropriate for what you are offering, go premium or invest in a completely original design. Big picture, big picture, big picture! And what about pricing? You need to be consistent here too, or first of all, that skepticism I just mentioned will bite you; and second, because you may lose out on leveraging different types of consumers.

It should be obvious that the font size or font color you use on your pricing page is far less important in terms of conversion, than is the presentation of a pricing plan that is consistent with your offering, and pricing that is competitively positioned. A lot of experts will tell you: "You need three different pricing plans, no more, no less, and you should make the middle plan the most obvious."

Seriously? Again, give people a little bit of credit. Who picks a pricing plan based solely on font size? If you are having conversion woes and can link them to your pricing page, and if some guru comes in and insists you fix your font, take a step back and ask yourself first: Are my pricing plans confusing? Uh-oh—they are! Then don't waste your time on tweaking your pricing page design— simplify your pricing.

If you've done all that—you know your pricing page design is solid and your plans are clear, but you still are struggling with conversion, take a look at your industry standard—how is everyone else presenting their pricing model? Is it helping you to stick with that same model, or might it be better to offer a much simpler one? For instance, if your competitors are offering three plans based on the number of users or licenses—how could you be disruptive? What if you decided to offer unlimited licenses at one fixed price—and raised that price just slightly? Always be thinking of alternate pricing models! A new pricing model might be just what a certain segment of the market needs right now.

Yes, as much as I hate to say it, and say it again, marketing is part science, part art, part luck. While some of the mystery has disappeared, some remains. We know humans are fickle, insecure, needy, wise, thorough, and loyal—we are all these things, both as marketers and as consumers. We are all doing the dance. We do everything we can to earn our customer's interest, we have them poised to hit that beautiful Buy Now button, but what makes them click? How do we rush them past any aversion to conversion, and become ours, and ours alone?

For each step of the funnel, you have to instill the appropriate kind of magic. And somehow, and this is the tricky part, you must never completely satisfy your customer's desire for better. You must never completely fulfill your promise. If you do, they will have no reason to take action. Continually create possibility; create more openings.

One principle stands above all others when it comes to leading your audience to take action: The promise that life is better after the click.

Dear Customer, All of your problems, or whatever particular problem you are having today, will be solved–if you simply click here.

Leave your customers wanting to know more.

In lead generation, if you only offer Request a Demo—it's not enough. Request a Demo is fit for those who have done their research and have already decided they are serious about your product. Be versatile. Be able to promise something else, like a great book, a white paper, or attendance at a webinar where a "celebrity" in your niche will give a short lecture. Better yet, provide an interactive calculator and ask people to feed in their own company data, then spit back out a result indicating if they are above or below their industry average. (Hint: The trick is to always have them come in under the industry average.) The data they just provided you? That's a lead right there.

eBooks, calculators, and webinars all fall under the realm of interest generation, but they play a part in lead generation too. These offers take a lot of work, creativity, and money—but if I had an unlimited budget, I would focus solely on creating these things. I would focus on creating the best string of never-ending questions and "mini-answers" or solutions as I could, in order to keep my customers clicking, turning my pages, and returning the next week for more. I would create as many opportunities as I could to teach them about my product and persuade them to spend more time with me— meaning, they would spend less time with my competitor.

I would be the worst best dating site character in the world— focusing completely on getting potential suitors to keep asking me questions about my glorious, useful, unique, honest, and life-changing self. I would use all the props the The Most Interesting Man in the World used, because there is a marketing spokesman who was so successful, Dos Equis is sending him off to impress Martians.

Chapter 11

The Ignored Marketing Channel

Retention and Fanfare: Where the Journey Begins and Ends

Someone once asked me, "What is the top thing about retention that keeps you up at night?"

I answered, "What keeps me up at night about retention is that retention is not keeping me up enough at night."

It's true: CMOs, and marketers in general, do not care nearly enough about retention. And fanfare? Most marketers will tell you that they are only supposed to generate leads, opportunities or generate sales—period. You must be kidding if you also expect them to handle retention. The pressure is always on the lead. That's the top KPI, and since you are always understaffed—with twenty salespeople waiting for you to feed them quality leads—that is what you obsess over. You think, "If I don't bring in the leads, retention and fanfare don't exist. End of story."

If you do want somebody that's good at retention, you need a specialist. And do you know who is great at retention, but often overlooked? Content marketers. Good content marketers know what makes people come back for more.

Now, of course, there are different levels of retention—and you won't need a content marketer working all levels. At the very basic level, you have to make sure that people use your product. You have to make sure they know how to use it, so this involves training, making sure the product has the right customer support structure, and so on. The next level of retention entails building recurring use—building stickiness into the product. How do you design product features that necessitate people logging back in or coming back for more? How do you encourage them to buy more of your product, or to upgrade or re-subscribe?

Sometimes you can do all of the above with something as simple and superficial as sending an email alert.

Then, there is the deeper work of marketing to existing customers. This is classic marketing work, if you will, to existing customers. And this is where you'll start to look to your content marketer, because as traditional as it is to tend to the people who already "Like" you on Facebook, you really have to up-your-game here. You have to find out what your existing customers need and create guides, eBooks, webinars, and special events for them.

Salesforce created Dreamforce. It is one of the largest conferences in the world. Who goes? Mainly, people who use Salesforce products.

Why does Salesforce hold the conference? One reason is that it gets their salespeople in front of their customers. Everyone learns about new products and features, and everyone walks away excited, and probably—further committed.

With Dreamforce, Salesforce is "thinking like a content marketer." They are boosting customer relations; they are delivering value and giving away valuable content; they are attracting the attention of their current customers, but are also expecting these customers to recommend them, share their content, and bring in people who are not yet their customers.

The likelihood of a salesforce customer who visits Dreamforce to purchase another SalesForce product is obviously higher than that of someone who doesn't.

To me, your clients are a marketing channel like any other. In fact, they are the very best channel available to anyone who has a critical mass of customers.

Just like social and SEO, your existing clients or customers are a channel you can cultivate and use to build retention and fanfare. If you are sending your existing customers the same newsletter you are sending to your prospects, stop. You are either completely understaffed or you're doing something completely wrong. Recognize immediately what your existing customers can do for you—beyond promising to come back.

This seems obvious, but surprisingly, marketers miss opportunities all the time when all it takes is a simple: "Hey, we're glad your department is happy with what we've been doing, but we are also interested in reaching out to other departments in your company. In our next meeting, we would very much appreciate if you could bring a few other departments into the conversation. Perhaps they'd be interested if we tacked on a certain feature."

The marketer's goal beyond happy customer, renewing customer— is, "I've got you covered, great! Now how can you help me get more clients?"

So you build a strategy. Beyond the question: What can this marketing channel of existing customers do for me, pose the questions to your marketing team: Could they do this for me, and how? Do I need a word-of-mouth recommendation? Do I want them to pass along information? Does our strategy provide some incentive to take action, like a coupon to share?

Clearly, you can't expect a bank client to break certain laws or a doctor to breach ethical barriers, but what *could* you expect of them?

When you ask your customers to go to bat for you, you've created a touchpoint. Identify different opportunities to create those touchpoints. For instance, the monthly meeting with the Logistics Department might not be a place where the marketer typically jumps in, but why not? Be disruptive: Create new touch points with your customers wherever you can.

It might benefit you to build your touchpoints into your contracts, where you stipulate that your customer will provide one recommendation every six months upon request that you will then post on your website as a testimonial. It might not be possible in your industry or with a specific product line, and it could be a deal breaker, but you won't know if you don't try.

Look at how MailChimp works. Buried in their contract and deep in their menu, there is a check box that most users don't even know exists, but it controls whether or not the MailChimp logo is attached to each of your outgoing emails. MailChimp is obnoxious in that this is their default "strategy," and it simply doesn't even occur to most people that there is a way "out," so they go along using the product and sharing the MailChimp name and logo with their friends. Even paying customers are still promoting MailChimp; I get dozens of emails a day from paying customers who have never deactivated that check box.

Is this aggressive? Yes. Is it effective? Absolutely.

The point is, you find and create touch points by giving customers something first—create an exclusive piece of content that by definition they would want to share. It's not easy, but this is how to support retention. As a marketer, think of retention as added value above and beyond the product itself. Think about ways of making customers feel good about belonging to this club of elite people, who are smart enough, for example, to use your brand of software.

In general, people are happy to help. If people are happy with your product, they want to share it. It makes them feel good. You just have to help them do it. In his books on persuasion, Robert Cialdini talks about the principle of consistency, which kicks in once somebody declares something publicly, for example, "I LOVE this product!" Once you have a customer who says this, they are resistant to ever publicly go back on their word. This deep human desire to avoid feeling stupid, or looking like a liar, is almost as powerful as signing a contract.

Marketers, take heed! You have to really screw up to have your fans turn on you. If you make them happy with your product, they will want to share it, in part because the act of sharing a good thing makes them feel consistent.

In sales school, one of the hardest truths for most people to swallow is this: Take your product, your brilliant product descriptions, your snazzy pitches and trade out your product with your competitor's. Everything still "fits;" it all "works." From the outside, we all have a competitor that does the exact same thing as we do—and they are cheaper.

One reason we are all basically sharing the same bed with all our competitors is that people often focus too much on the product itself. The product may have become a huge hit because of performance, but when it comes down to it, many times I've seen companies that could achieve better KPIs—better in terms of investment—if they would either downgrade, or hire somebody to replicate their product for less. The product might be designed to be of high-usage and dynamic, but the way it is being used by actual customers, means it could be very easily replicated without all the bells and whistles.

As CMO, when I see this happening, I try to shift the focus away from *all* the features of a product, to precisely which features customers are using and showing interest in. For example, if a company creates software that *could* perform two-dozen functions, but their happiest customers use only three of them, I'll say, "Let's build more content marketing around the three functions your customers are using, talking about, and evangelizing."

Again, we can look to Cialdini's principle of consistency here: Somebody might wake up this morning and say to himself in the mirror while shaving, "Oh, I've been wasting my company's money five years now. I think we could do better with a cheaper product," but nobody actually wants to speak these words out loud. The rationale behind maintaining the status quo could be maintaining the departmental budget, it might be "bad timing," it might be simply inconvenient or uncomfortable to stay abreast of newer technology and sleeker more efficient models. The freshly shaven man drives into his office with all the best intentions to make a move that could improve his product and ultimately improve retention, but decides while pulling into the company lot: "Nah. We'll just stick with the familiar."

Not that sticking with the familiar is always bad. Nothing in marketing, nothing in business, is inherently bad or good. It's just that if you are approaching a client with a "Hey, hey, look here! I've got something new for you," but their motivation is stability, you're losing your key advantage. It pays to grow your intuition; it pays to speak to customers on their level. Try to have some idea what their expectations are before you ask them, "Are we meeting your expectations?"

Everybody knows there's a lot more money in existing clients. Existing clients are far easier to sell to than potential clients. But in a tragic paradox, most of my marketing peers admit: "Yeah, but we don't really focus on that."

The truth is that most vendors, most manufacturers, and most marketers don't have the option of staying in touch with their clients. They work really hard to try to, but with retail, the buyer disappears—

you never knew who it was anyway. At this stage then, marketers don't talk about paying attention to their clients, but about loyalty.

Airlines offer rewards, car dealerships offer free service for a year, razors offer replacement blades, shampoo companies offer refills—and in this way, even if the marketing team has no way of paying attention to each and every customer, they have created the illusion—that is, a system—where the customer comes back for the same thing over and over again, for years and years.

Loyalty is about creating an emotional engagement with people, even if that engagement is as distant as can be. It is about creating top-of-mind awareness and the perception that there is something to gain from loyalty. The benefits may save customers just a few bucks here and there, but the emotional draw is in the illusion of saving time. Consider women and lipstick. If a woman decided ten years ago she'd found a brand and a color that everyone complimented her on, she is sold! Forever! She doesn't have to do any more research: Fashion may change, her skin and hair may change, but she doesn't have to keep asking people, "Does this color lipstick look good on me?"

What is the true benefit of staying loyal to the brand of lipstick? It's a mix of many, but saving time and effort is definitely up there on the grand scale of things.

Apply this concept to bigger ticket items—you may be furious with Apple or with Microsoft, or with your phone service carrier, but are you really going to go through the hassle (and cost) of switching?

Building and maintaining loyalty traditionally has been hard, but it may be getting slightly easier, thanks to the experience economy.

With the rise of customers using multiple devices, comes more opportunities for brands to make new touchpoints—for example, via apps. This is a real evolution in the grand scale of marketing, and most brands are not doing much with it—yet.

Here we go with another toilet paper example! Charmin's SitOrSquat app helps customers find clean public toilets. Instead of wondering how to push toilet paper on people, they asked how they could a build a relationship and create value for people. It's brilliant! If I think Charmin cares about my hygiene, I'll appreciate it; but more importantly, every time I'm on the road and need to do my human business, Charmin will be at the top of my mind—it doesn't matter if I am actually standing in the toilet paper aisle ready to make a purchase, or not. When I am standing there, what will likely be the first toilet paper brand to come to mind?

Apps that appeal to recipe collectors work in a similar way: "Make this delicious caramel-flavored latte with our brand caramel."

Creating meaningful moments that people love to curate and share is the big revolution, and yet very few are working this revolution to the max—like Red Bull is. Everybody talks about Red Bull, they rule the experience economy. They are almost so good that they turn even people who are not their customers into fans of sorts.

Think about it.

I might not drink Red Bull, you might not drink Red Bull—but I could be just as loyal as the guy who drinks Red Bull morning noon and night if I find one of their campaigns sexy or rock-and-roll or somehow expressive of what I stand for—high energy, enthusiasm, youth.

If a company gives me tools to express my "fandom," I might just use those tools. Maybe, again, I don't drink Red Bull but they offer up some app about Ibiza and I enter as a "Red Bull Fan" there—shopping for my next vacation of the 24/7 party life! With music too, I can mix and "produce" my own songs, sampling from artists I may never buy more than one clip from, but if I use that clip and share it with thousands of people, I've become a fan to some degree. I elevate the original musician.

We marketers try to determine who our fans are, where they are, and what motivates them to be our fans? Who loves us? You do? Oh, then please love us more! And then please go on and on about how much you love us to all the people you love!

We marketers are kind of pitiful that way. It's hard to discover what demographics love you. If you are not in a position to collect a complete list of all your fans, ask yourself, who hates you? What an opportunity! Do not try to please all of the people all of the time. Take a stand that is so strong and so authentic and so true, people will talk. Some will love you, and some will hate you. Having haters is a good indication that you have fans out there too! Emotion is your friend and your frenemy—tread fearlessly and openly. Stay disruptive, my friends.

Chapter Twelve

Send Me Hate Mail

If You've Got No Haters, You've Got No Lovers

Throughout my long career in marketing, I've pissed a few people off and have experienced a couple total failures, but there is one particular hater I recall. By today's standards, one might not even call her a hater, she certainly wasn't a troll. But, she got under my skin by comparing me to a used car salesman. Ouch! Let's call her a hater.

(It's true, isn't it? A thousand people may love us, but it is the one who insults us, cuts us down, and belittles the work we do, that we obsess over. Marketers—let us consider it a part of our job to figure out which of these haters are worth hearing out and turning around!)

Anyway, this particular hater came to me years ago, via email. I had created a system to move a product, and that product started off at a very high price and was then offered at extremely steep discounts.

"Why are you selling this product this way?" my hater began. "You're no better than a used car salesperson. I don't trust you, and now I don't trust your product. I'll never buy from you, ever!!!" (Haters always use three exclamation points.)

When I shared this feedback with my team, a few were shocked and a few got rowdy; but, we all felt unethical all of a sudden. We felt bad about ourselves. We *did* stop to think about what she'd said. Ultimately, we looked at one another and shrugged: "But, hey, that's our tactic. Okay so the 'Act quickly/one day only' message doesn't appeal to this person? Too bad!"

We decided then and there that if the pendulum had swung far enough for one person to hate us, it meant that somebody else loved us! We checked our emotions: Should we really feel like slimy bums here? In fact, are all used car salesmen really slimy bums? NO! Let's keep going!

Marketing doesn't work if you stay right in the middle. You have got to go to some extreme and push hard, to some end, with your messaging and style.

The point is never to purposefully offend anyone, but to be controversial. It's a fine line and you will cross it occasionally, but be a marketer—own it—live on this edge.

I love the people who love me, but I love my haters too. I don't believe I have failed when I'm hated. I believe I've engaged people. Nothing is worse than apathy. Nothing is worse than being mediocre, or even, good enough. The challenge is not dealing with people who find fault with you, your company, or your brand. The challenge is keeping your team going when emotion hits—"Don't like our 'today only special' style, then maybe you are not for us.'"

This does not mean you'll encourage your team to purposefully garner and nurture hate, no, it means you'll encourage them to withstand it, to test if it is relevant, and to respond accordingly. You want a team with permeable and flexible creative muscles, but thick skin. As long as everyone on the inside is *with the program*, they will not be swayed by love or hate from the outside, they will do their damn jobs—they will keep their eyes on the funnel, the content, and the journey.

If you lead with compassion, you teach compassion. This trickles down to the journey you take customers on. The woman who didn't appreciate the "act now" way I was selling a product was not the customer for me, and besides, there will always be haters. Certain Amazon product reviewers would find fault with a gold toilet (fine, I won't bring us back to toilet paper again).

We're not looking for hate and we never ignore criticism. If someone tells us our product sucks or we are acting like a used car sales team, we stop and look at two things: Is this our ideal customer? Is this the type of person we are trying to attract? If so, we did something very wrong. This will happen from time to time, and we will take steps to improve things.

If, however, we determine our hater is the type who would likely never buy our product to begin with, we thank them (internally) for verifying that we are on the right track. We communicate to them something like: You're right. This product/this company is not for you. We suggest you try Company XYZ."

We are helpful, always.

When you attract the wrong audience, take the opportunity to learn from it! What did you do that you shouldn't have? Did you advertise to them, or make promises that were relevant to them? If you are a luxury hotel, and somebody complains about your "ridiculous" gold toilets, did you accidentally put out an ad for 99% off—attracting Motel Zero buyers?

Most marketers afraid of getting hate mail—not me. I imagine that for every piece of hate mail I receive, there are at least 5X the number of love mails out there, they are just never written. I imagine this love mail, and I keep going. I then tackle my hate mail.

Engagement is key.

If the hater of this book is, in my mind, a traditionalist, or a growth hacker—or simply the type of marketer who claims they use a bunch of little tricks that sometimes work, and sometimes don't—great. I invite everyone to keep on doing what they're doing. If you know it all already, as you were, Sirs and Madams!

What I'm describing in this book is not for everyone. There are certain markets where there is no reason to be disruptive, or no possibility to be disruptive. I do not seek these markets out; I do not engage. I play the disruptive game when and where I can, and have a damn good time.

In situations where I can see I don't have as much money, talent, and experience as my competitor, my ONLY way of winning the game is to be more disruptive. In fact, if I can rely on the fact that the Goliaths already know how to do what they do so well, I can count this off as perhaps their only weakness. If my disruption catches, they don't stand a chance.

Will disruption always catch? No. Will you always attract some haters? Probably.

Embrace them. Recognize the fundamental urge of every single one of us to be loved and to feel a part of something bigger than ourselves. If your hater is truly a potential customer, shake hands and make up. Think politics, think schmooze, hell, think make up sex if you want— but ultimately, recognize the drama for what it is—it is *so human.*

In this book, I'm doing my best, but I'm also inviting you to dislike, critique, criticize, or hate what I've written. What do you stand for? What is your vision of marketing? If it differs from what I stand for and envision. Send me your hate mail, I'm sincerely curious.

And if it seems too much work for you or you think I'm not even worth getting upset about, here's a template I encourage all readers to complete and email, Tweet, or post on Facebook:

_____ Daniel,

Your book was _____ pile of _____. It was a _____ of my _____ time. I am definitely not a ____ of your ideas. In fact, your ideas should be called _____, or maybe, _____. I'd like nothing better than to invite you to give a lecture at my university next month though, so that people can throw _____ at you while you _____ on stage. Disruption is for _____!

Sincerely,

How Did I Even Get This Far?

About The Author

Daniel Glickman is an internationally recognized marketing leader, speaker, and writer. As CMO of Roojoom, a customer journey management solution provider for B2C brands, he builds and manages digital marketing, advertising, and PR activities. His blog, newsletter, and international Meetups—all under the title CMOConfessions—offer a frank, creative, and humorous take on the underbelly and undercurrents of today's most pressing, exciting, and confounding marketing issues.

With over two decades of experience in marketing, sales, and brand promotion, Glickman is known as a leader who is committed, charismatic, and "profoundly creative." He enhances communication across teams and drives customer-centric processes to create new sales channels, disrupt markets, and help build highly profitable companies by leading the marketing department to "own the P/L".

Glickman combines his deep knowledge of marketing technologies with a creative approach to marketing and team-building. He is able to listen to clients' needs and pare complex systems down to facts and data. As a result, he specializes in integrating and transitioning companies and teams seamlessly across all levels, while simultaneously delivering what clients need and propelling profits.

He currently lives with his wife and two children near Boston, where he enjoys sailing, cooking, writing, and disrupting marketing and sales meetups whenever he can. He's a fan of asking and answering difficult questions and has been accused more than once of reeking havoc.

Contact:

Email: Daniel@cmoconfessions.com

LinkedIn: https://www.linkedin.com/in/glickmandaniel

Facebook: https://www.facebook.com/cmoconfessor

Made in the USA
San Bernardino, CA
21 November 2016